THE USEFUL BOOK OF

GADGETS, GIZMOS

& APPS

THE USEFUL BOOK OF GADGETS, GIZMOS & APPS

Solving life's little problems, one gadget at a time

Martin Bailey

Management Books 2000

2000

First published in 2016 by Management Books 2000 Ltd
36 Western Road
Oxford OX1 4LG
Tel: 0044 (0) 1865 600738
Email: info@mb2000.com

Web: **www.mb2000.com**

British Library Cataloguing in Publication Data is available

ISBN 9781852527723

005·3

Contents

Introduction

As an unashamed geek I'm often asked (or just volunteer information) about what my weapon of choice might be to solve a particular problem – whether it's charging a phone on the move, how to stream music and videos around the home or the best app to recover deleted files. When friends and family visit the conversation inevitably turns to technology.

I grew up in the 1980s as a 'Sinclair child', selling my Scalextric racing car set to buy a Sinclair ZX81. Those were genuinely exciting times and I felt that my generation was on the edge of something amazing. The internet took that to a whole new level, with most people now connected and relying on it daily, directly or indirectly.

There has never been a more exciting time for gadget-lovers. The average person has a smartphone in their pocket that is thousands of times more powerful than the computers that put man on the moon, and the 'Internet of Things' promises to connect to all areas of our lives. Health-trackers are aiming to keep us living longer, while there are 1001 gadgets that try to entertain us and make our lives just that little bit easier.

This book aims at solving life's little problems, one gadget at a time. It's designed as a short and succinct read that you can pick up and dive into quickly.

I'd like to state that I have not been paid in any way to promote any of the products in the book, nor do I have an affiliation with any of the manufacturers or retailers. Many of the items covered in this book I actually own and use. The rest are gadgets that I'd either recommend to solve a particular problem, are just plain innovative or simply just quirky enough to make it into these pages. The appendices at the rear are also included for a little fun, showing the most extravagant, extreme and in some cases obscene gadgets available.

Remember that although I've selected the items in this book they may not be 100% suitable for your own needs, they may have been upgraded or even ceased being manufactured by the time you read this. A small number of gadgets were undergoing crowd-funding at the time of writing, and while I've been very selective about choosing campaigns that were close to or had surpassed their goals there is always a risk that even if successfully funded the product may never actually see the light of day. At least now that you're aware of them you can use the Internet to find alternatives or similar gadgets that might work better for you. Google is your friend! When you've found a gadget and are shopping around for the best price a good tip is to enter the product name/code into your search field and add the word 'review' after it. You can then view all of the product reviews online to ensure that you make the right decision. Although I've quoted prices they may have changed significantly by the time you read this book.

As a side-note, if you want to install any software or mobile apps covered in this book do take a moment to check that you're running a compatible Operating System (OS). These days a mobile phone can expect to receive updates in the first three or four years of its life, after which you'll find that as new apps are released they may not work on an older OS. Worse still, if you decide to erase your device (perhaps to give it to a family member after you've upgraded) you might find that you can't even download apps that you previously had installed, as the latest versions are no longer compatible with your OS. Planned obsolescence is unfortunately a fact of life with technology as manufacturers crank out new devices each year – they have to give us all a reason to upgrade.

I hope you enjoy reading this book as much as I've enjoyed researching and writing it. If you have a gadget to recommend then please use the contact form on my website at **www.theusefulbookofgadgets.com** to let me know. Alternatively, if you find any of the gadgets useful or find an innovative use for one again do get in touch.

Dedicated to my raison d'être – Mia.

Other books by Martin Bailey

Marketing your Business (1st & 2nd Editions)
Learn to use a PC in 90 minutes
Building a website using a CMS in 90 minutes (1st & 2nd Editions)
Get more visitors to your website in 90 minutes

Recover accidentally deleted files

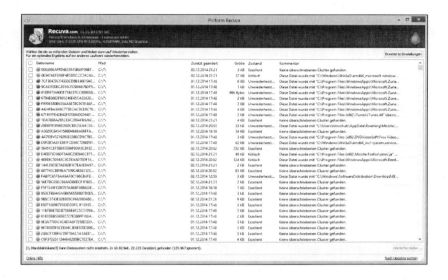

Most people have lost files at one time or another, but sometimes it's possible to recover them, even if you've formatted a hard disc. I had a neighbour that had not only wiped the disc, but also reinstalled Windows on top of it, and I was still able to recover 70% of their lost photos, including some of their new-born child.

When files are written to any form of storage media, whether it's your hard disc, a USB stick or a memory card in a camera, a log is written to what's known as the File Allocation Table (FAT) or the Master File Table (MFT). When you delete a file the reference to it is removed but the physical file remains on the drive. It's like removing a line from the table of contents in a book without removing the chapter. Just because you cannot see it does not mean that it's not there!

There are various programs, both free and paid for, that can scan your drive and find/recover deleted files. The app I used on my neighbour's laptop was *Recuva* from Piriform. The standard version runs on Windows, is free and provides a simple wizard-based process to run a scan in just a few seconds. A deep scan takes much longer – sometimes several hours, but can often find older files. You can also do custom searches, such as searching for images deleted after a certain date. This is especially useful if you've just made a mistake and are using *Recuva* to rectify it, as the search and resulting file list will be much shorter.

More importantly, if you are handing a computer onto someone with the operating system still installed but want to make sure they can't restore any files you can also permanently erase them after you've used the app to identify what could still be recovered. *Recuva* does this by writing zeros over any previously deleted files.

A 'Pro' version is also available with automatic updates and more advanced features, such as support for virtual machines. There's also a portable version that runs from a USB stick – see also the Portable Apps page further in this book.

Top Tip: Install this app now, before you actually need it, so you have it ready to run the moment you need it. The more you use a PC after disaster has struck, the less chance you have of getting all of your data back, as Windows is constantly writing temporary files to the hard disc, possibly overwriting the very files you are trying to restore! Even powering down and rebooting a PC will reduce your chances of recovering files.

There's a reason this app is first in the book – it's saved data for me more times than I'd care to admit. So grab it, install it, forget about it and then thank me when you need it.

 More info: www.piriform.com

Charge your phone anywhere

We are increasingly reliant on our phones. In addition to being essential communication devices they are our diaries, phone books, cameras, news sources, timepieces and entertainment devices. Consequently the necessity to charge them is a constant worry. Enter the *Nomad Key*, available in both Micro USB and Apple Lightning formats.

This tiny USB 2.0 device, measuring just 6.6cm long and weighing in at 7g attaches to your key-ring, allowing you to charge your device wherever you can find a USB port, which these days is an increasing number of places.

The Lightning version is Apple certified, meaning that it can also be used as a syncing cable. This is important to note, as many low-cost cables available from online retailers are only capable of charging iOS devices and cannot be used for data transfer or, more likely, they'll work for a short while before displaying a message stating 'this accessory is not compatible with your device'.

The micro-USB version is suitable for most USB devices, including current Android, Windows and Blackberry phones and tablets. There are also no issues with data transfer on the USB version.

Nomad also sell the Carabiner, which is in the shape of a belt clip if you're looking for something a little more rugged. In addition, the company has also branched out into other battery and charger products including a wallet with a built in battery and cable, so it's worth taking a look at their website.

Couple one of these with a portable battery and you'll never have to worry about running out of juice again. You'll also be very popular with your friends when you're out and about and their battery percentage is low.

I've used one of these now for over a year and have lost count of the times that this has saved me or a friend from that sinking feeling of single-digit battery percentage.

The *Nomad Key* was funded successfully on crowd-funding site Indiegogo, raising over $172,000 in 2013, exceeding their target goal of $50,000 by 345%!

At the time of writing you can pick up the Apple Lightning version for $19.95, with the Android micro-USB version slightly cheaper at $14.95.

 More info: www.hellonomad.com

Track a stolen laptop

If you've ever had the misfortune to have a laptop, tablet or phone stolen you know that it's not just the loss of the hardware that's the problem. What about your data? What about all those sites that you've saved passwords for so that they automatically log you in? The portable nature of laptops means that they are often backed up less frequently than their desktop counterparts, putting your data at even more risk.

Fortunately there's the *Prey Project*, a software product available for Windows, Mac, Linux, Android and iOS. Once installed it remains invisible and dormant until you report your item as stolen via their website. If your laptop, tablet or phone is subsequently connected to the internet you can receive an alert, see its location, view a screenshot of what they are doing, activate the webcam to take a picture of its new 'owner' and even lock down the device so that your data is safe. You can also flash up a message to state that the device is stolen.

The basic version is free for up to three devices and allows up to 20 reports concurrently being stored for each, with paid-for accounts providing more report storage and further functions such as remote device wiping. You can stick with the free account and choose to upgrade if the worst happens and your tech goes astray. At $5 per month covering up to three devices it certainly doesn't break the bank and is a small price to pay if you can retrieve your device.

Their website has plenty of success stories to demonstrate that it works, and at a starting price of free there's no excuse not to have this running silently in the background. Some of the stories are quite amusing, with various webcam snaps taken on stolen tech definitely not safe for viewing at work, with the victim often managing to turn the tables on the thief by threatening to go to the police and publish the photos unless they return their ill-gotten gains!

As a side note you can protect your kit more effectively in the first place by ensuring that you at least have a password to unlock it. Don't forget also that many mobile devices have remote tracking pre-installed and the capability to remotely wipe the device as standard.

 More info: www.preyproject.com

Turn furniture into a wireless charging port

Most of us need to charge at least one device overnight these days, which leaves us with multiple wires trailing from bedside cabinets and plugs fighting for sockets. The end of cables is in sight, however, with more and more phones being equipped with wireless charging capabilities, but if your handset does not support it there may be a simple solution.

Furniture companies such as Ikea are not only providing products such as tables with built in wireless charging points, but they also sell wireless chargers that you can easily integrate into your own furniture. Furthermore they even sell cases for all current popular brands of mobile phones that don't yet have wireless charging built in.

Assuming you want to customise some existing furniture, you simply purchase the *Jyssen wireless charger* for about £30 and cut a 77.3mm diameter hole (very carefully!) in your existing furniture.

What is particularly nice about the design is that you can pass through other cables, such as for a mouse, and pressing the unit down fractionally forces it to raise, giving access to a USB port.

If you own a phone that does not support wireless charging you can simply buy one of their cases for selected phone model. The case will connect to the power socket on your phone and can then be placed on top of the wireless pad for charging. They are priced between £10 and £20.

If you don't rate your DIY prowess enough to let yourself loose with an electric jigsaw on your table and you don't want to replace your furniture you can always purchase one of their single or triple charger pads (available in white or light wood colours).

If your tech supports wireless charging then these little upgrades are a great way of removing the myriad of wires and chargers from bedrooms, kitchens and living rooms.

 More info: www.ikea.com

Keep your PC running like new

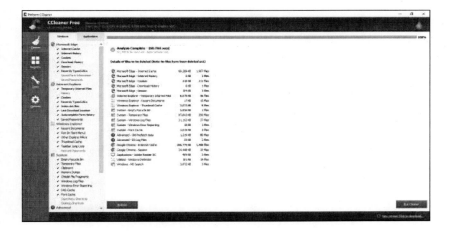

As you use your computer Windows can have a habit of getting slower and slower. Applications often create temporary files which remain on your drive long after they were used, taking up valuable space. Files such as cookies that are downloaded as you browse the web can track your behaviour online to serve up tailored advertising. Finally, the most common cause of a slow PC are the 'helper apps' that silently start in the background each time you boot your PC.

CCleaner (the C stands for 'Crap'!) by Piriform provides a number of functions to help keep your PC running sweet while also freeing up hard disc space. The tool you'll use most frequently will be the main cleaner app. After selecting the files and apps you want it to clear, with all the main ones ticked by default, just click Analyse to see the amount of space each one is currently taking up. Once the analysis is complete, which can take some time if you've not run it in a while, just click Run Cleaner to zap those files and instantly reclaim often gigabytes of space! I'd bet hard cash that the first time you run this you'll save several hundred megabytes, or maybe gigabytes.

Next up is the Registry Cleaner. Windows holds a database called the Registry which contains various settings relating to the operating system and apps. As apps are installed, used and uninstalled, the Registry can get cluttered with information that is no longer required, and *CCleaner* does an excellent job of removing this. In my experience you won't see much of a speed or space improvement here, but on a slower PC it may be the difference between mildly painful and dire!

The tools section has a variety of smaller but no less useful apps. In addition to an app uninstaller, duplicate file finder, drive wiper and disc analyser there's another hidden gem with the System Restore option. Each time updates are installed Windows takes a snapshot of all core files, called a System Restore Point. Each snapshot is often several gigabytes in size. *CCleaner* allows you to view these files and delete all but the last one. Personally I'd recommend deleting all bar the last two, just in case an app installed just before an update is causing you problems. Also take a look at the Startup tab to see what apps are starting on bootup or when you open your web browser that you could perhaps do without. If you're not sure whether to disable something do a quick search for 'should I disable X', or take a look in the *CCleaner* forums.

Available in free and Pro versions for Windows, Mac and Android, as well as a portable USB version, *CCleaner* is an app that I'd recommend regular PC users run at least once or twice a month. After running this, why not also run a disc defragmenter, to move all of your files to the start of your drive (unless you have a newer SSD drive, which does not need this) – on an old system you could quite easily save gigabytes of space and see a significant speed boost.

Whenever a friend asks me to take a look at their slow PC this is the first app I turn to in order to remove the irrelevant before I start to work on the relevant, and it can really breathe new life into a PC that hasn't seen much technical love in a while.

 More info: www.piriform.com

Never lose a password again

With each week bringing a new horror story of an online security breach it's never been so important to take control of your own security measures, so let me ask you this: How many websites do you use the same password for? Chances are that most people are using the same username and password combo for multiple sites, which means that if one company gets hacked the bad guys only need to try all the major online stores with the same login details in order to strike it lucky.

There are a variety of password management tools available, but the most simple I've used is *LastPass*. Firstly, create an account with a nice long password. Make sure that you will remember it as *LastPass* state that if you lose it they have no way to retrieve it! Install the plugin for your favourite web browser and click the new icon in your browser toolbar to log in. Once signed in, each time you either create a new account or log into a web site you'll be asked to save your credentials to your 'vault'. Next time you boot up your PC and log back into the *LastPass* browser plugin it'll automatically populate any saved login fields with your data. You can even configure it to auto-login, entering the details and submitting them. It also has a handy password creation tool, which I use to create unique 14 digit passwords for every site I visit.

In addition to storing usernames/passwords you can store other data, such as credit cards, billing and shipping addresses or notes. You can even attach documents or images to notes, ensuring you always have a secure digital copy. I recommend using this to store copies of documents such as passports and other important files, which you can then access securely from any internet device should you need to.

If you use it on a newer smartphone with fingerprint recognition this takes the simplicity of it to a whole new level. You can open a website on your phone and use your fingerprint to instantly log into any sites that you've stored on your PC.

Even though *LastPass* themselves were hacked in 2015 the encryption level they use is so high they confidently stated that there was no risk that anyone's passwords would get into the wrong hands as even they don't have access to them.

Once you've built up a database of your most popular sites you can also take their 'security challenge', where they check to see if you have easy-to-guess passwords or commit the cardinal sin of the same password across multiple sites. You're given a simple percentage ranking at the end, with a detailed list of what needs to be done to improve your score.

LastPass is free for use on a single device or can be used across multiple devices for a low annual fee of around $12. If you use a lot of websites across different devices then I think it's a small price to pay to provide peace of mind without compromising on usability. *LastPass* is available for Windows, Mac, Linux, Android, Blackberry and iOS, as well as a variety of different browsers.

 More info: www.LastPass.com

Charge your devices and jump start your car

Portable batteries that you charge via USB and then use to top up your devices on the go have been affordable for some time – whether it's a phone case with a battery, or handbag-friendly chargers only a little bigger than a lipstick. The *JunoJumper* from Juno Power, however, packs another trick up its sleeve – it can jump start a completely dead car battery!

In addition to being able to charge smartphones, cameras and tablets via its 6000mAh battery that provides a 5v 2.1amp output, it can also deliver a 12v output at a peak rate of 300amp.

The *JunoJumper* is packed into a case a little larger than a 5" smartphone, has a micro-USB socket to receive charge and delivers its output through a standard USB socket. It also includes a handy LED torch. Four LEDs on the top of the unit indicate how much charge it's holding. It does take a few hours to charge, but as we all have our nightly charging routine with devices it's just one more to add to the list once it's been depleted.

Juno Power reckons that the fully charged unit will completely charge an iPhone 3-4 times, and can jump start a car of up to 2L engine size.

It's not cheap at over $100 when you compare it to batteries with twice the capacity, but you only have to use it once to restart a flat battery for it to pay for itself – both financially and emotionally! It's small enough to sling into a bag and gives you that extra feeling of security when travelling.

 More info: www.junopower.com

Check your heart rate without a fitness tracker

Many people now track their heart rate while exercising, often purchasing dedicated heart rate trackers such as Nike Fuelband or Fitbit, but did you know that your trusty mobile phone can track your heart rate as well?

Apps such as *Instant Heart Rate*, available for iOS, Android and Windows Phone, use the flash on your phone. Start the app and press your index finger gently over the flash and camera lens. The flash lights up, highlighting the blood as it moves through the veins in your fingers. Today's mobile cameras are sensitive enough to be able to pick up the changes and map a real-time photoplethysmogram (PPG) graph of your heart rate on screen in a matter of seconds. Once the reading is complete you are also asked to specify your current active state, e.g. resting, post-workout, etc., which then goes to build up a history log. You can also add notes to each log, and can add tags to show what you were doing at the time you took the reading.

Bringing in the social aspect, the app also allows you to view a real-time heart rate map across the world, so you can get a sense of how truly unfit you are on a global scale! It's compatible with *Apple Health*, and can pump all your heart data into it.

The basic app is free, with premium services and in-app purchases including medical grade reporting and a stand-up test that analyses your heart's strength based on how hard it has to work when you stand up. Premium also allows you to export your data for use in other applications.

Some of the testimonials include people that have identified heart conditions which have successfully been corrected, and although you obviously need to be able to understand the data the app presents to you, it's still a very useful tool to have in your pocket. Over the next ten years we will see a massive surge in fitness tracking, perhaps to the point where your phone notifies you hours or days in advance of an impending serious health issue that can be dealt with before it occurs.

 More info: www.azumio.com

Never lose data again

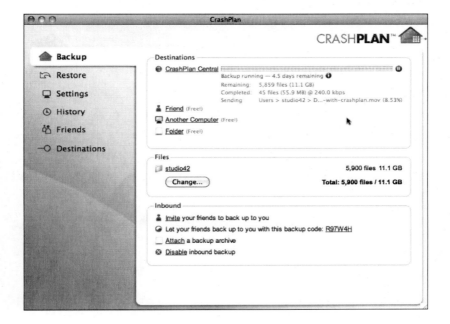

We've already covered software that can recover data after it has been deleted, but what about those times when the hardware simply isn't accessible, either because of theft or failure? Even with the best of intentions, most of us are not disciplined enough to back up our data regularly.

However, with continually increasing broadband speeds online backup is now a viable alternative. There are many companies that offer the ability to silently and constantly backup your files in the background, and *Crashplan* is one such offering. Sign up to the free 30 day trial, download the desktop app for Windows, Mac or Linux and specify which folders you want to backup, and then just sit back and relax. *Crashplan* will then transfer your files to its 448 bit encrypted secure servers. As you save files they are updated on the backup server, with each version kept. This means that if you realise that you made a mistake on that spreadsheet three weeks ago you can roll back to a version prior to the mistake. You can even configure it to keep versions going back over years.

To my mind this is a much better solution than an external USB hard disc that you occasionally plug into your PC. Firstly, the backups are constant and incremental, but more importantly it's a protected location, meaning that should your computer be affected by, say, ransomware (where all of your files are encrypted and the hacker demands a ransom to unencrypt them) all you have to do is remove the ransomware by formatting your drive and reinstalling your operating system and then restore your files.

The app itself does have a free option – it will allow you to specify a different computer to back up to, such as a friend's. The warning here is to make sure that if you're the selected friend, you have room on your PC to store the backup data, which can run to terabytes if you're not careful! Also, if you are on a metered data plan you could find that you quickly blast through that before you've downloaded anything yourself!

I recently had occasion to thank *Crashplan* (again) after deleting files accidentally and bypassing the recycle bin (which you can do by holding down Shift when you press delete). The files could not be recovered using file recovery software, but *Crashplan* had dutifully backed them up moments after they were created and kept them in its servers, even though I'd deleted the source files.

Crashplan offer a variety of monthly subscriptions starting at $5 per month for an individual computer but my recommendation is on the $12.50 per month for up to 10 computers. Both plans come with unlimited space, and mobile apps are also available, allowing you to download files on the go. There are those that have lost data and those that will lose data. I do not intend to be in the latter group ever again.

 More info: www.Crashplan.com

Add lyrics to all of your MP3 files

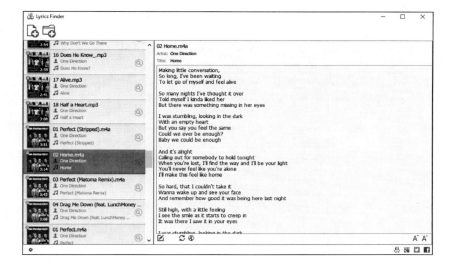

We've all been there – either trying to remember the lyrics to a song or arguing with someone over the correct words. Lyrics are freely available online, so those arguments can be generally resolved quickly, but you can also quickly add lyrics to all of your MP3s. These are stored as 'metadata' within the MP3 file itself along with information such as the artist, track name, album name, etc. When you subsequently sync them with other devices such as phones and tablets the lyrics are available there too.

If you were to try to add lyrics manually this would be a very laborious task. Using a Media Player such as *iTunes*, select a track and view its properties (in *iTunes* that means right-click and select View Info). You'll see one of the tabs is titled Lyrics. You'd have to find the lyrics for each song and then copy/paste them into the dialog box for each track.

I found the free *Lyrics Finder* app from Media Human to be particularly easy to use. Once downloaded (for either Windows or Mac) you select your files and folders in the left window. The app immediately scurries off, locates the lyrics and adds them to your MP3 files without any further input required from you.

The process of adding lyrics requires your library to be well structured. By that I mean that each file should have artist, track and album information stored within the file itself so that it is correctly laid out in *Media Player* or *iTunes*. If you've purchased music online through legitimate sources or 'ripped' your CDs using software such as *iTunes* or Windows *Media Player* (which then connects to the internet to match your CD and automatically embeds all track names), then there should be no problems. If, however, you've just got a collection of MP3s that do not have any embedded artist and track information then no lyrics will be added.

The first time you run *Lyrics Finder* on your library it may take some time, especially on large collections but after that whenever you run it the software will ignore tracks that already have lyrics and then only spend time populating any recent purchases.

Lyrics Finder is a great way to add a little bit more polish to your music collection, and may just impress your friends slightly down the pub when you're able to instantly display the lyrics for any track for the music collection on your phone.

 More info: www.mediahuman.com/lyrics-finder

Download anything from *YouTube*

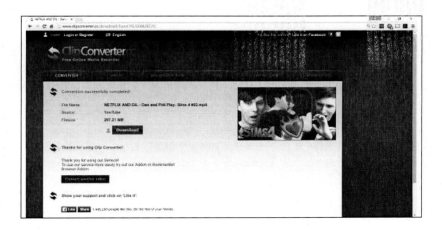

Everyone is partial to the odd meme or cat video on *YouTube*, but there may be times when you want to get your *YouTube* fix but don't have internet access. Or perhaps you've uploaded a video to a video site yourself but have lost the source files and want a convenient way of downloading it again. The same also applies to audio.

There are various websites that will allow you to copy the web address of a *YouTube* video and download it as either a movie file or audio-only MP3 file. I've listed *Clipconverter*.cc, which gives you the flexibility of downloading either, but note that sites like this often go offline, so you may need to find another similar online service. A quick search for 'download *YouTube* video' will provide plenty of alternatives.

The process is very simple. Bring up the video you want to download on *YouTube* and then select the full URL in the address bar at the top of the page. Copy this to the clipboard using CTRL & C, or right click and select Copy. Now browse to the video/audio grabbing site of your choice and paste in your URL where prompted by either right clicking and selecting Paste or pressing CTRL & V. The website will then recompile the *YouTube* video as a downloadable file, often providing you with different resolutions and file formats on the next page. Usually MP4 will be the best format for you to select, as this will play on most devices.

Important: Many videos are free to download, but a lot of content on *YouTube* is copyrighted. Please check the video details text to see if any copyright or licensing information is listed against any videos that you wish to download. If in doubt do not download as you may be breaking the law! Some videos may not even download if additional copy protection has been applied, so bear that in mind if you encounter any errors.

If you try to use a site that prompts you to download and install some software in order to subsequently download/convert your video then avoid it like the plague. It is possibly laden with malware or other such nasties.

I've found *Clipconverter* invaluable for downloading a couple of videos that I'd lost the source files of, and it's certainly a very simple yet useful tool to be aware of.

 More info: www.Clipconverter.cc

Scan all of your business cards

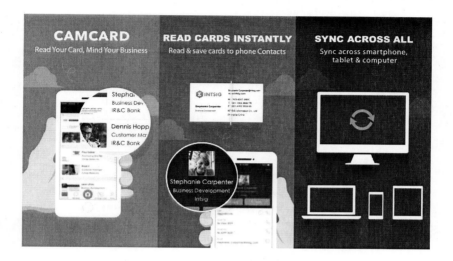

If you are in a job where you tend to collect business cards you'll know how difficult it is to remember details about each person. During a trade show, for example, you'll meet dozens of people and end up with a stack of cards. Many companies put so much effort into these events only to end up with a stack of cards and no notes relating to the people behind them. As a result the money spent on the event, often tens of thousands of pounds, is nowhere near as productive as it could have been if all of the leads were properly catalogued and followed up.

An app I've sworn by for a number of years is *Camcard*. It allows you to scan a card and, using OCR (Optical Character Recognition) coupled with some very clever software, it will read all of the text on the card (in 16 different languages) and drop it into relevant fields such as phone, fax, email, address and job title. It's not 100% accurate, so you'll need to quickly glance over the results and dip in if any corrections are necessary, but it does a pretty good job probably 80% of the time. If the card also has a rear image you can add a photo of that, and you can even associate a photo of the person with the card.

Once you've scanned and verified your data you can create folders to store them within the app itself, which is very useful. I use this to categorise cards by event. You have the option to search within a folder or your entire database.

After saving to the *Camcard* database you can also choose to save them to your phone's contact list. Importantly, you can also add notes to each card, so you won't forget any details of your meetings. This is actually one of the most useful aspects and should not be underestimated, as any text you entered in the notes field is also searchable, so the more you write the more effective your searches will be.

Camcard also gives you free syncing to their servers, allowing you to access or export your contacts at any time through their website and sync across multiple devices. Losing your phone and not having a backup would not be a problem for your *Camcard* records – just log back into your new phone and all of your records will sync back down again.

What takes this app to another level is the sharing capability. As well as being able to share cards you've saved with others you can also add in your own cards which can be shared just as easily – very handy when you run out. Often at a trade show I will scan a card that is of relevance to someone else and share it within minutes of the meeting ending.

Camcard is available for all major mobile phone platforms and also has a plugin for *Microsoft Outlook*. At under £2 it's an absolute must for business users.

 More info: www.Camcard.com

Never lose an online auction again

The likes of eBay brought auctions to the masses with many people using the site to make a living, but for most of us there will probably have been an auction where we paid over the odds to secure a product.

Online auctions are timed, so the most important moment is the last few seconds. The last bidder wins, and they only have to pay a small increment over the previous bidder in order to potentially snap up a bargain. The balancing act is in placing your closing bid as close to the auction end time as possible while also resisting the urge to just place a bid too high for anyone to match.

There is another way – snipe them! Sniping is the process of placing a bid automatically in the closing seconds of the auction at the next price increment, based on a pre-determined maximum price that you are prepared to pay. As long as the auction ends at an amount lower than your ceiling and nobody else has a competing snipe placed later than yours, then you are almost certain to win the auction.

There are plenty of free mobile and web-based apps out there, but they are normally limited to a couple of free uses, after which you will pay a small fee for each further snipe, which on lower cost items will impact on the savings you make. I found a low-cost app which, after purchase, is totally free to use. *Auction Bidding Sniper* by Picture Engine Company has a simple four-stage process. Start by logging in with your eBay username and password, and then go to an auction that has an end time. Enter the maximum amount that you are prepared to pay and click the Add to Snipe button. A few seconds before the auction ends the software will check the highest bid and, if lower than your specified amount it'll then place the next incremental bid.

There are versions of this app for Mac OS and iOS, but no Android or Windows versions so you'll have to look to other vendors for other platforms. The only downside of this app when used on iOS is that you have to keep the app open (e.g. keep the screen switched on) in order for the snipe to be placed as it cannot bid when the app is in the background. My recommendation would be to set a reminder shortly before the auction closes and place your snipe then, ensuring that you stop your phone from locking.

I've won many an auction using this app, ensuring that I don't get drawn into a bidding war and only pay what I'm comfortable with. If you're a collector and are trying to bid on that elusive item then this is an essential app for maximising your chances of winning without blowing your bank account. You can pick up the Mac OS app for around £2.50 or under £1 for the iOS version.

 More info: www.pictureenginecompany.com/ BidSuccessOSX/BidSuccess.html

Remove spyware from an infected PC

We are at constant threat from malicious software – whether it be via email attachments or 'drive-by downloads' from infected websites. While antivirus packages will do a good job of stopping many threats they can often miss malware, which can work very differently to traditional viruses.

There are many free and paid-for products available, but one that has consistently worked for me is *Malwarebytes Anti-malware*. Downloaded over half a billion times, *Malwarebytes* can successfully remove many of today's threats.

For clarity *Malwarebytes* is not antivirus software as such, but it can catch many different types of viruses. A virus is a piece of code capable of copying itself in order to do damage to your computer. Malware is a general term for other malicious software that go by such names as worms, trojans, spyware, adware, ransomware, etc., but it does also include viruses.

Many of today's viruses employ stealth techniques to avoid antivirus software. *Malwarebytes* actually turns the tables, including its own

'Chameleon' technology, protecting it against attempts to disable or modify it.

What I particularly like is its ease of use. After downloading and installing the main program it will quickly check online for any updates to its malware database, which are released regularly. One click on the large blue button starts the scan, and that's it. Now go and make yourself a coffee, as this will invariably take a while. Once completed you'll see an overview of any threats and be prompted with recommended courses of action. Normally the default actions are fine, so clicking Apply Actions will then fix any issues. Essentially that's two clicks to keep your system safe.

Malwarebytes provide security software for Windows, Mac and Android devices. There's a free version available, along with a Premium version for around £20 that provides additional functionality. You can also run it in Premium mode for a 14-day trial period, allowing you to use some of the more advanced features to clean up your PC (as well as testing the version for possible ongoing use if you decide to sign up).

I'd recommend a two-tiered approach to your antivirus and malware security. You should always have an antivirus package running at all times on your system. That'll take care of viruses in emails or files. Having a regular regime, perhaps weekly, of running *Malwarebytes* will ensure that your system is free of any nefarious software.

 More info: www.Malwarebytes.org

Run all the apps you'll ever need from a USB stick

There are times, perhaps when you are travelling, when you may need to access software and data but only have access to insecure computers such as at Internet Cafés or a friend's computer. Maybe you need to write a document, edit an audio file or even process video. There are online tools that will do many of these tasks, but if you don't have internet access your options are limited.

I've included many apps in this book that can be run from a USB stick without needing to be installed, and there are literally hundreds of apps that can be stored and run from a single stick. Imagine having a complete office suite, antivirus and conferencing software such as *Skype*, web browsers, encryption software and much more all in your pocket – for free. With high capacity USB sticks so cheap you could also include all of your documents, pictures and music as well.

Portableapps.com is a downloadable platform that effectively installs a menu system onto your USB drive. From there you can select and install from over 300 apps. You won't find paid-for apps on here like *Word* or *Photoshop*, but there are plenty of open-source alternatives that will meet most users' day-to-day needs. When you plug in the stick it auto-runs and places an icon in your system tray which, when clicked on, displays something similar to the Windows Start menu. Any files that you place on the drive are accessible to the right using an interface similar to Windows Explorer. Apps can be organised into folders or favourites, and the built in search box allows you to quickly find what you're looking for.

It's essentially like having a completely portable PC that you can take with you anywhere. None of these apps need to install onto the host computer – they run entirely from the USB. You can also install apps to cloud services such as *Google Drive* or *Dropbox*, keeping everything in sync and accessible across different devices.

There are also several antivirus and PC repair/security products available, so for security alone it's a very prudent idea to install them on a stick and keep them available for when you really need them.

Portableapps runs on Windows, Linux, Unix, BSD, etc., via Wine and Mac OS using products such as Crossover or Wineskin.

 More info: www.Portableapps.com

Keep tabs on keys, remotes, bags, etc., as well as your phone

Chances are that at some point, possibly at regular intervals, you've misplaced your keys or your phone. Or perhaps you are prone to leaving your handbag or glasses case in another room?

There is now a very neat solution to this frustrating day-to-day problem. Tile tags are small square trackers that can be either attached or adhered to everyday objects. It's supplied with an app for either iOS or Android and uses Bluetooth to connect to your phone. You can connect multiple *Tiles*, each of which can be named. When the inevitable happens just fire up the app, select the Tile you want to locate and wait. If the Tile is within around 30m (100 feet) it will play a loud noise until you find it. The app also records the last time and place that it located your items, which is useful for example if you've left a bag in a shop.

What's very cool, however, is that this also works in reverse. The Tile has a single button. Double tap it if you've lost your phone and it'll force your phone to ring – even if it's on silent. Furthermore, if it's out of range you can log into the *Tile* website to see the phone's last location, make it ring or send a lock screen message. In fairness, most people won't need this as they will most probably have dedicated apps on their phone such as Find my iPhone on iOS, which also has the ability to remotely wipe a stolen handset, but it's a very quick way to reacquaint yourself with your phone when it's playing hide and seek down the back of the sofa.

The *Tile* itself is very low-maintenance, with the replaceable CR2032 battery lasting around a year. It measures 37mm square and 5.3mm thick, which is about the thickness of two keys, yet the tiny speaker emits a 90 decibel tune when activated.

The *Tile*'s search capability uses the power of its growing customer base, as if an item is lost and is out of range of your phone it only has to come into the range of any other Tile user and it's whereabouts will be updated instantly (without telling other users where your lost goods are). There are dozens of 'lost and found' stories on the Tile official website, so this is clearly a solution that works.

Priced at around $25 each they are not cheap, but you can get discounts if you bulk buy, which is ideal at Christmas for all of your absent-minded friends.

 More info: www.thetileapp.com

Turn your phone into a photocopier and filing system

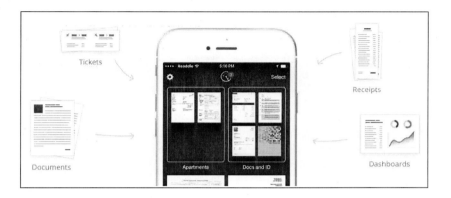

It's quite common now to take a picture of any documents you want a digital copy of with your smartphone, but this has a few drawbacks. Firstly, any documents are lumped in with all of your other photos. It also means that anything sensitive could be brought up on screen if you are browsing through your library, perhaps with friends. More importantly, it's difficult to create copies of multi-page documents.

I've been using *Scanner Pro* – an app for iOS only – for several years now, and it is by far the most useful app on my phone. It doesn't just take a photo of a document – it will find the edges, remove shadows and use 'keystone' correction to deliver you a perfectly cropped image to the same shape as your document, regardless of whether your phone was squarely above it. If you're scanning a book it'll even straighten out any curves in the scan. You have the option to save in full colour, greyscale or black and white, with the latter two options significantly reducing the resulting file size. You can also rotate pages as required. After only a couple of taps you can take further shots, quickly creating multi-page documents saved in PDF or JPG formats.

Scanner Pro allows you to create folders to store your documents, all of which are searchable. This is incredibly useful on its own, but when you connect the app to a cloud service and set it to automatically sync each time you scan something this becomes its killer feature. For example, I have a folder within the app for receipts. For every purchase I make I'll pull out my phone, snap the receipt and it'll be instantly uploaded to my *Dropbox* account, which in turn means that the receipt is synced to my PC within seconds.

The inclusion of Optical Character Recognition (OCR) means that you can scan a page and convert it to editable text. This is especially useful if you need to rework a printed document but don't have the source digital file – just scan and OCR it and within seconds you can copy/paste editable text.

The app takes full advantage of iOS's sharing capabilities, allowing you to email or print with a quick tap or open scanned documents in other apps. You can also create 'workflows' – sets of instructions such as 'scan, create PDF and attach to an email' with just one click.

Security is also well taken care of. You can set a password, or use *Touch ID* to unlock the app when you open it. This makes the process of taking a scan incredibly quick – less than 10 seconds, in fact.

In addition to getting rid of years of paperwork such as wage slips I also scan passports, flight, hotel and insurance documents when I travel, so if I lose the originals they are not only on my phone but also synced to my *Dropbox* account, accessible from any internet-connected PC.

Scanner Pro is an absolute steal at under £2. If you're on other platforms such as Android or Windows there are plenty of alternatives, but spend some time to make sure that they have features such as folder creation, password protection and cloud syncing. Most of these types of apps have a free, limited functionality version to allow you to see if it meets your needs, so it's worth downloading a few to see which one you feel most comfortable with.

 More info: www.readdle.com

Keep your tech safe and charged on the move

As we carry around more and more tech it's important to make sure that it's well-protected. Fabrics have advanced significantly over recent years, providing a breathable, lightweight, water-resistant shield, with more tech-friendly designs providing a sleeve for laptops or tablets.

There's a wide range of rucksacks that will take a laptop, but it's worth researching a little further based on your own tech needs. For example, if you also have to carry, say, a DSLR camera, then there are rucksacks that can accommodate the camera body and a couple of lenses along with a 15" laptop. If I'm travelling for an overnight business trip I tend to need room for a laptop, 10" tablet, external hard disc and the relevant power supplies, along with a fresh set of clothes and toiletries.

The other consideration nowadays is power, and with rucksacks they fall in two camps – battery packs or solar panels (that charge battery packs). The type you choose will generally depend on how you want to use it. If you're the festival-goer type then solar might be the best option but for the most part a rechargeable battery will suffice.

The *Energi+ Backpack* by TYLT is a rucksack designed purely for tech, comprising of a 10,400mAh 4.1A battery capable of charging three devices simultaneously and has the capacity to charge a smartphone four times. There's a trolley slot behind the rear panel, allowing it to slip over the handle of a suitcase, and 13 pockets in total. Cables can be routed to any one of the five external pockets or two internal pockets.

It's not cheap, at around £150, but it's hard to beat it on flexibility. You may be able to combine a much cheaper rucksack with a decent battery pack, but again do your homework based on your gadgets and travel requirements.

 More info: www.amazon.co.uk

Turn an old smartphone into a security camera/ baby alarm

If you upgrade your smartphone every couple of years or so there's a good chance that you have an old but perfectly functional handset languishing in a drawer somewhere. Why not breathe life back into it by turning it into a security camera? This is useful if you're away from home and want to keep an eye on pets or property, or perhaps want to use it as a baby monitor while in another room.

There are many different apps available in all app stores, but one of the better ones I've seen is *AtHome Camera* from Ichano. The basic app is free, with upgrades to a Pro version and a monthly cloud-based video recording option also available.

There are three steps to getting it up and running. Firstly, download the Streamer app on the device that will be used to stream from, e.g. your old phone. Next, download the Camera app that you want to use as a viewer onto your new phone. Open the app, sign up for free and log in. Finally, add your camera using the displayed unique 'CID' code or the QR code and you're instantly connected with a video and audio feed.

This app includes a number of advanced features, including motion detection with email or 'push' notification, scheduled recordings, two-way talking and pan and tilt when used with supporting camera. Some of these require the Pro version, but at around £6 it's not going to break the bank. It works over either Wi-Fi or 3G/4G connections, but note that streaming video for any length of time over 3G/4G will eat into your data plan.

The fact that it works with a complete mixture of iOS, Android, PC webcams and even third party IP-based security cameras makes this a good all-round app and an excellent way to add security to your home, or to work as an ad-hoc baby monitor. Don't forget to keep the phone plugged in and powered up though.

Note also that there are some more fully-fledged security systems that will also allow you to integrate an old phone as part of a wider network of security cameras. So you might choose to install professional exterior cameras but recycle an older device for use indoors. Now that you know you can re-use that old phone it's just a case of hitting the search engines to find a solution to meet your needs.

 More info: www.ichano.com

Get a better SATNAV for your car

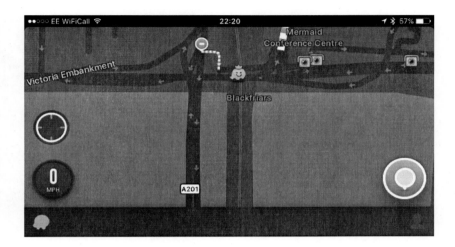

I've always been underwhelmed with the in-built SATNAVs of many cars, even more premium brands. They are often run on underpowered hardware making them sluggish to use, have poorly thought out interface controls and, most importantly, are either difficult or costly to update. More advanced features such as live traffic updates or speed camera locations are sometimes not as advanced as they appear, are expensive additions or often not even available.

Although it may seem like overkill to use your phone as a second SATNAV, once you install this next recommendation you won't go back. *Waze* is owned by Google, and is available for iOS, Android and Windows devices. In addition to harnessing the power of *Google Maps* it also crowd-sources live traffic information. Other 'Wazers' are shown on the map as icons, giving you an indication of the fact that you are looking at real-time information constructed on a global scale. If *Waze* detects that you are in traffic it will update other users instantly, automatically recalculating the estimated time of arrival. Users can report events as well, whether it's a vehicle stranded at the side of the road or a police speed trap hidden round the corner. No other SATNAV system can give you this degree of 'finger on the pulse' information.

Whenever I've used this app it has been the most efficient at re-routing me around problem areas, often before I've been notified on my in-car SATNAV or have heard about the problem on the radio, and it's predicted ETA has never been more than a few minutes wide of the mark.

Waze includes a social aspect, allowing you to send your journey progress to friends to let them know your current status and arrival time and even sharing local fuel prices, saving you money by routing you to the most cost-effective vendor en-route.

The best thing about *Waze* is that it's free. I've been mildly annoyed by the ever-so-occasional advert for things like fast-food chains or restaurants en route, but the adverts are very infrequent and have always been relevant to the journey rather than for a plumber local to a road that I'm never likely to drive down again.

 More info: www.waze.com

Keep your boiled water hotter for longer

The kettle is one of the highest wattage items in your home, perhaps aside from the washing machine or iron. However, we often waste power on it needlessly, heating more water than we need and then re-heating it again and again when we want another cuppa.

To put it into perspective, a 60 watt lightbulb used for an average of five hours per day will still cost about a third less than a kettle boiled for a total of just fifteen minutes per day.

A British company, *Grunwerg*, based in Sheffield, has combined two tried and trusted technologies – a kettle and vacuum flask. Once you seal the lid a vacuum is created which keeps the water so hot that even after four hours it's still at around 68 degrees C. Also, as the lid is closed during the boiling process there's no steam to curl your wallpaper. The base is fitted with a temperature gauge, allowing you to set a temperature to heat the water to, which is useful if you want to infuse delicate herbal teas which would be otherwise destroyed at higher temperatures.

There are a few relatively minor drawbacks – it's heavier than the average kettle, at about 1.6kg, and it takes a little longer to boil, but this is offset by the fact that you have to boil it less frequently. There's also no fill indicator on the side (as that would inevitably dissipate heat). If energy-saving and the convenience of hot water is your thing then these are small compromises to make.

Expect to pay around £65 for their 1.5-litre kettles, with higher capacities also available.

 More info: www.grunwerg.co.uk

Manage, edit and backup your photos

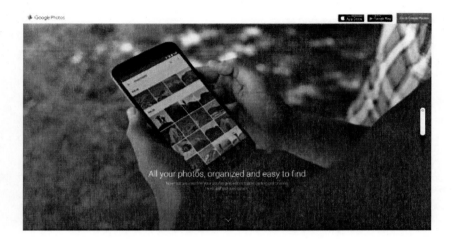

With everyone packing a half-decent camera on their smartphone and many of us already having a significant library of digital snaps taken with pocket or DSLR cameras we can quickly end up with a large collection of photos which are difficult to manage. Also, high-end image-editing packages such as *Photoshop* are expensive and complex to use, especially when you only want to crop, straighten or perform basic adjustments to an image. They also say that in the event of a fire people run for their photo albums – that's a bit difficult when they are spread across one or more computers which are also at the mercy of theft or mechanical failure.

Google previously offered its excellent *Picasa* software, but retired it in March 2016 to only offer an online photo-editing solution – Google Photos. While it does not have as many features as *Picasa*, Google Photos does offer (and deliver) an excellent way to sync and backup all of your photos across all of your devices.

For starters, Google will provide you with unlimited storage space for your photos if you save them in their standard resolutions – 16 megapixels for photos or 1080p for videos. As only professionals are likely to be shooting at higher resolutions this is a no-brainer. If you are a purist and want to cherish every pixel forevermore then you'll have to stump up some cash and purchase a Google storage plan.

Start by downloading the free Google Photos app for whichever device you want to use. They offer PC, Mac, iOS and Android flavours. I'd recommend installing it on all of your devices to really reap the full benefit. Open the app and log in with your Google account (or create one for free) and it'll scurry off and start uploading your photos. While the mobile apps provide you the means with which to view and navigate your library the PC app only handles file uploads, so you'll have to go to photos.Google.com in order to view and manipulate your snaps.

Once you're in either the app or web page you'll immediately be presented with all of your photos in descending date order. Use the scroll bar to move down by date or use the creepily good search facility to search by place, date, object (e.g. cars) or, if you enable it and tag some photos, by person. There are two other views – Collections and Assistant. The Collections screen contains albums, movies and stories (with stories being a visual timeline of photos and videos). Assistant periodically automatically creates movies or animations based on your recent uploads. If you like what you see you can save it to your library and share it with others.

When you view a photo, a series of buttons at the top right of the screen allow you to share, edit, zoom, delete or add the photo to an album. Editing functions are basic, but do the job. They include automatic or manual adjustments of brightness and contrast, a variety of filters and the ability to crop and rotate. You can also download the image to the device that you're on. Being Google, sharing photos is easy, with links to the likes of Twitter, Facebook and G+.

To my mind this is the first app you should download to a PC or mobile device. Having a service that will automatically backup and sync all of your photos – forever, for free and across all devices – is an absolute no-brainer.

 More info: https://photos.Google.com

Block annoying/dangerous popups when browsing

The internet is awash with advertising. Remember – if you are not the customer you are the product. Sites need revenue to survive, so if you are not paying to view content on your favourite news site, for example, then expect to see advertising wrapped around content.

Some advertising is annoying but safe – *YouTube* often shows an advert before a video that you can skip after a few seconds, and overlays adverts during playback that you can close, but others are more sinister. Visit many software download sites and you'll be presented with several adverts that look like the link to download the software you've searched for, or, worse still, they will disguise themselves as Windows popups, warning you that your PC is infected and inviting you to 'scan your system'. Clicking the link instigates a download of software whose purpose is often not only to get you to pay for fake antivirus software, but also download/install other malware. In extreme cases you may get hit by 'ransomware' – software that encrypts everything on your PC and requires you to pay a ransom in order to get the decryption key.

Ad Block Plus is a free plugin for most popular browsers that works silently in the background, stopping ads from loading. Its Open

Source nature means that it has a thriving community developing and improving it. Installation is simple. Visit the website and it'll detect your browser, offering you a link to install the plugin. A couple of clicks later and it's installed and working.

In addition to blocking ads, complete domains known to contain malware can be blocked. Many web pages will have small areas that are actually web pages loading from an entirely different server. If that server is on a blacklist then *Ad Block Plus* will ensure that it is not shown. It can also disable tracking, both from general ad agencies and social media sites. Have you ever been surprised by an advert on social media when you were shopping for the very same product earlier? If you are logged into Facebook and visit a page that has Facebook 'Like' icons, Facebook will know that you have visited this site and serve up appropriate ads on your next visit to them accordingly.

Of course, many websites rely largely on advertising revenue, and *Ad Block* respects this, publishing what it calls the Acceptable Ads initiative. Any ads that adhere to their guidelines of being non-obtrusive will not be blocked. So any ad that is deemed to be in an appropriate position or size will not be blocked. You can also disable *Ad Block Plus* for specific domain names altogether if you wish.

Although many websites now detect when a blocker is in use and respectfully ask you to disable it to help sustain their business my argument is that by installing products such as this you are adding another layer of protection against the darker side of the Internet.

 More info: https://adblockplus.org

Turn a tablet into a second monitor

Tablets are great. They provide a quick-access gadget that allows you instantly to check email, jump on the web or watch your favourite TV show. Since the *iPad* was launched in 2010 tablets have become omnipresent, with most households owning one and today's children only ever knowing a world with 'pinch to zoom'.

However, when the kids are at school you can put your tablet to another use – a second monitor, providing an extended desktop. You might say 'I can only look at one screen at a time', but studies show that workers are around 30% more productive with a second screen and I can certainly confirm that from personal experience.

I've used two screens for my desktop PC for some years, but this wasn't really feasible when I was travelling with a laptop – until now. There are a small number of apps for tablets that will essentially turn them into a second monitor, allowing you to either mirror content from your main screen, which is ideal for presentations, or extending your desktop (perhaps allowing emails to be on one screen while your main app is on the other). *SplashTop XDisplay* is the best I've found to date, offering two apps – one that uses your USB cable to transfer the data and the other using Wi-Fi. I opted for the wired version, as when travelling access to a Wi-Fi network is not always guaranteed, which would then mean no second screen as well. Note that the wired version will also charge your tablet, thus shortening your laptop's battery life – this may be a problem if you're in an airport lounge with no plug socket in sight.

To get started download the free 'streamer' app for either PC or Mac, and then download the app for iOS or Android. There's a free time-limited tester app, with the full paid-for version costing around £6. The Streamer app runs silently in the background on your main computer. Opening the app on your tablet will instantly connect and share your screen. You can then configure it exactly is if it were a real monitor. You can change resolutions or move it to the left-right of your main screen (so that it matches where you physically place the screen). Don't expect to play games though, as there is a small but noticeable amount of lag, which might be more prominent on a slow wireless network, but for static content such as email or web pages it's perfect. You'd want to leave movies for your main screen as well.

With most of the major tablet manufacturers now offering super-sized tablets this might be the compelling reason you've needed to buy one. The standard-sized 10" displays are a little on the cramped side, but the newer, larger tablets are comparable to a 13" laptop display.

 More info: www.splashtop.com

Learn a new language for free

Many of us often dream of owning a place in the sun overseas, but language (aside from the cash) is often a barrier. Night school may not be an option for busy households or for those on shift-work, and CD-based learning may feel a little out-dated.

Duolingo is a free website that allows you to immediately jump into one of over a dozen languages, including French, German, Spanish, Italian, Russian and even Esperanto. With over 100 million users it is now officially the most popular way in the world to learn a new language online – and this has been achieved in just two years.

Lessons are presented in a simple, graphical format, with audible representation of the words on screen so you also get to learn the pronunciation. Each section differs between text, pictures and audio, so you get a healthy variety of content to keep you interested.

You can complete the first lesson without registering, just to get a taste, after which point you'll need to create a free account to store your progress. Once the simple registration process is complete you can dip in and out as your time permits. Your progress is remembered, so you'll start exactly where you left off each time you reconnect.

There are also apps for iOS, Android and Windows Phone, so you can continue your lessons wherever you are and on whatever device you have with you.

According to an independent study an average of 34 hours of *Duolingo* are equivalent to a full university semester of language education. Since a one-semester university course usually takes more than 34 hours of work, this study suggests that *Duolingo* is more effective than an average university course.

What I particularly like is that this is something you can dip in and out of very quickly. If, for example, you have a few minutes spare in the car before you pick the kids up from school you can get a section or two completed. So now there's no excuse not to tick off that bucket-list item of learning a new language. Why not see what you can do before your next overseas holiday?

 More info: www.Duolingo.com

Stream music to your old music system

With the advent of MP3 players and now streaming the hi-fi system, possibly with a turntable on top, may have languished in a corner of your living room for some time. Now there's an easy way to quickly 'cast' whatever's playing on your PC, tablet or phone to an older-style device.

In 2013 Google launched its *Chromecast* HDMI device that turns any TV into a smart TV, and in 2015 they launched an audio version. This small puck-shaped device is similar in design to its video counterpart and can plug into a 3.5mm, RCA or optical socket on your music system or active (powered) speakers. A 3.5mm-3.5mm cable is included, but you'll have to purchase the other cables if you need to connect to RCA or optical.

It is powered through a standard micro-USB socket and connects to your Wi-Fi network using an app for iOS or Android. Essentially it acts as a bridge between your old music system and your digital music using Wi-Fi. As some music systems have USB ports this could even be used to power your *Chromecast*.

Once you've followed the simple setup process you're ready to cast. There are dozens of apps that already support *Chromecast*, such as

Spotify, Deezer, Vevo and *Tunein Radio* to name but a few. A notable exception of course is Apple, but iOS users can download the Google *Play Music* app and sync up to 25,000 songs to the cloud for free, which can then be streamed by the app.

Where this starts to really make sense is if you have multiple *Chromecast*s in different rooms in the house. You could perhaps start the day streaming music in the bedroom, switch to the kitchen and move onto the living room, casting to different systems at the touch of your smartphone. Another great feature is that you can also configure a Guest Mode, allowing friends to stream music from their devices without even being connected to your Wi-Fi network.

The *Chromecast* Audio device is a great alternative to more expensive speaker systems available, taking full advantage and breathing new life into your existing equipment. Another benefit is that it does not suffer from the relatively short distance limitation of Bluetooth audio. At £30 it's also an absolute steal.

 More info: www.Google.com/intl/en_uk/Chromecast/ speakers

Build your own Media Player

If you have a relatively large household you might have a collection of photos, music and video spread across different computers. Playing these on your main TV can often be a bit of a problem. Or maybe you use a computer as your main media device and want a single piece of software to navigate all of the above? There are plenty of devices on the market that claim to offer the capability to bring all of your media together but they usually either come at a price or with additional baggage – namely tying you into their ecosystem (such as *Apple TV* or *Amazon Firestick*).

Enter *Kodi*, formerly known as *XBMC*. It's an Open Source (and therefore free) Media Player that supports all major audio, video and image formats. In addition to displaying whatever is available locally on the SD memory card or an inserted USB stick it'll also stream anything on a local network and even from Internet locations. It'll basically play virtually anything you throw at it.

The interface is slick, with what the developers call a '10-foot' sliding interface that slides left to right, designed specifically for TVs and remote controls. If you are not keen on the interface you can re-skin it, with dozens available. Furthermore, there are hundreds of add-ons covering audio, video, weather and more. You can also link it to other apps, such as *Media Portal* to turn it into a PVR, recording live TV.

What is astounding about *Kodi* is the number of platforms that it can run on. Windows, Linux, Mac OS, Android and *Raspberry Pi* are all supported. (iOS is supported, but only on 'jailbroken' devices). You could install *Kodi* on a PC or laptop in about a minute and plug it straight into the HDMI socket on your TV for an instant and free media centre. Also, if your TV remote conforms to the HDMI-CEC standard then, with the right IR (infra-red) hardware on your *Kodi* device it'll control that as well.

To my mind it's the *Raspberry Pi* option that's the most interesting, and actually not that difficult to set up. The *Raspberry Pi* is a sub £30 computer not much bigger than a credit card. You can download an installer that will install *Kodi* to a micro SD card for your Pi in just a few clicks. Insert the micro SD card, connect a cheap wireless keyboard and then connect it to your TV – you now have a small yet powerful Media Player that can be tucked away and can connect to all of your media wherever it is stored. There are plenty of tutorials online that will take you through all of the steps of building it yourself – start by visiting the *Kodi* 'wiki' area on their website, and also search for *YouTube* videos on your chosen OS platform. With a vibrant online community and the system being developed since 2003 it's a very mature, stable, supported and well-documented system. There are also plenty of different case designs for the Pi available, so you can tailor it to fit your living room.

If you like the look of *Kodi* but don't want to tie up your PC or build your own unit you might want to turn to Amazon or other online stores and purchase one of the many Android-based *Kodi*-powered media centres that have sprung up. These are pre-loaded, supplied with a remote control and ready to run for around £30-40, but do check the reviews as some devices can be underpowered and lead to a lacklustre and 'laggy' experience.

 More info: www.Kodi.tv

Run other Operating Systems on your computer

There may be the odd occasion where you want to run an old piece of software that's no longer compatible with your current OS. Perhaps you want to try some software or even a different operating system without risking your main computer setup? Alternatively, maybe you want to have a way to run your entire system on another computer easily.

A virtual machine (VM) is essentially a computer within a computer. You can create a completely 'sandboxed' environment where an Operating System can be installed inside of your own system but without interfering with it whatsoever. Imagine double-clicking on an icon like an app, and then a window with Windows running within it starts up – that copy of Windows thinks that it is running on its own computer and does not 'see' your computer. You could, assuming you have a computer powerful enough, have multiple different operating systems running side by side simultaneously.

VirtualBox, by Oracle is one such application, distributed under an Open Source license and available for Windows Mac OS, Linux and Solaris operating systems. Download and install it, and then start the virtual machine creation wizard. Allocate some of your computer's resources such as memory and hard disc space and then specify the OS that you intend to install. Next, have your OS installation CD handy, or download the OS (usually in an .ISO file format) and point the virtual software at the disc/file. Your new OS will install as normal, but within its own ring-fenced 'box'. It will exist as a single file on your computer that you could then back up and run on any other computer with the same VM software.

Virtual Machines are a great way to play around with other operating systems such as Linux, many of which are also free. I also find it useful to have older copies of Windows installed, in case I need to test something.

As a side note I once had a very entertaining 30 minutes with a scammer who called my home, reportedly from Microsoft, saying that they had 'detected that my PC was spewing viruses out onto the Internet'. I allowed him to connect to a virtual machine running Windows XP where he then spent half an hour trying to convince me that my machine was riddled with malware and that he could sell me the solution. I then informed him it was a virtual machine and unsurprisingly he hung up! I then deleted the virtual machine, safe in the knowledge that it could not possibly damage my main PC in any way.

 More info: www.VirtualBox.org

Stream videos to multiple devices anywhere

"Are we there yet?" are the words that any parent dreads on a long journey. Portable devices such as phones and tablets have largely resolved this issue, aside from one problem – movies. If you have a large collection of digital movies you may not be able to fit them on a tablet, and what if the little darlings each want to watch different movies on their own devices?

Someone had the bright idea of combining a portable hard disc with a battery pack and a wireless router to give you a self-contained pocket-sized device that can hold hundreds of movies which can be streamed wirelessly to multiple devices using its own Wi-Fi network, with the battery providing several hours of cable-free operation.

There are several companies manufacturing such devices. I've selected the Seagate *Wireless Plus*, which is available in capacities up to 2TB capacities. The built-in router allows up to 7 devices to connect wirelessly for up to ten hours (although if you are constantly streaming you can expect considerably less in my experience).

It also supports other streaming technologies, such as DNLA, Samsung's *Smart TV* and Apple *AirPlay*, making it an excellent all-round solution for both the home and car. Plug in the supplied USB cable and it will operate as a standard external hard disc for your laptop. It uses USB3, and can therefore backup all of your data pretty quickly too.

There are also a couple of internet-related features that I've found useful. Firstly, it can piggy-back off of your own Wi-Fi network, giving it Internet access, which is useful for updates to its own software. Secondly, you can link it to either *Google Drive* or *Dropbox* and keep an entire backup of your cloud-based content on the drive. This can be really handy if you need access to a file in your *Dropbox* account when you are away from your own computer and have no Internet access.

Seagate offers Android and iOS apps to allow you to browse the content wireless. Start by switching on the drive and waiting about 30 seconds for the in-built router to boot. Once the blue light goes solid, open your device's Wi-Fi network setup and connect to the network as you would any other wireless network. Once done, start the Seagate app and after a few seconds your files will be displayed, grouped as videos, pictures and audio. One caveat is that some devices may not support the video formats within the Seagate app, so you might have to download another Media Player or convert your source videos.

These types of drives are not cheap, with the 2TB setting you back around £140 – that's twice the price of a standard external hard disc, but for all-round functionality on the go it cannot be beaten.

 More info: www.seagate.com

Make a quick floorplan using your phone

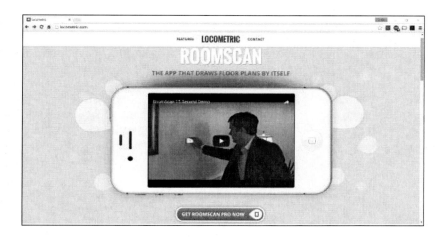

Measuring up a room for flooring or furniture is a tedious job, especially when measuring irregularly shaped rooms, but yet again your trusty smartphone can come to the rescue.

Roomscan from Locometric is for iOS only (although there are similar products for Android) and uses the sensors within your phone to quickly scan a room. You start by placing the phone against a wall, waiting for a beep and then moving to the next wall or window and repeating the process. As you move around each contour of the room the plan magically appears on the phone. The room is complete once you've covered all walls plus the first one a second time, which effectively 'closes the loop'. Wall lengths are associated with each wall and these can be manually adjusted if you do decide to use either a traditional tape measure or laser measuring device. It can also be paired with some high end laser measurers to drastically improve accuracy

Once you've drawn the basics you can then add in doors to complete the room. As you scan further rooms they can be added to create an entire floorplan of a property. You can save an image of your plan to the Camera Roll for free but if you want to export to another format such as PDF, DXF or DWG then you'll have to stump up to purchase credits, however with 50 export credits costing under £1 it's hardly going to break the bank and will certainly be of value to anyone that uses the app regularly.

Another great feature is that you can associate notes with a plan. *Roomscan* can even take photos and place them in the correct position on the plan.

Priced at around £4, the developers suggest that the app is accurate to within 10cm, so if you are measuring up for new furniture and are tight on space you might want to either back it up with more traditional methods or invest in a Bluetooth laser measurer. Most of the reviews on the *iTunes* App Store appear to be positive, and my own experiences back that up.

If you're in a trade where you have to regularly measure a room or even if you're purchasing your next home this is a great app to help quickly create a complex floorplan.

 More info: locometric.com

Install multiple apps on a new PC at once

I usually end up reinstalling Windows on my PC every 12 to 18 months – sometimes sooner if I am unlucky. Aside from the installation process and subsequent download of hundreds of security updates the process of installing all of those useful little apps that I've picked up along the way adds to the overall tedium of the process, and I generally forget one or two apps as well.

Ninite.com has helped to alleviate a significant portion of this. It's a very simple idea – the website stores installers for many popular free apps, including (but not limited to) *Chrome*, *Skype*, *iTunes*, *Spotify*, *VLC*, *Java*, *Paint.net*, *Libre Office*, various antivirus packages, *Dropbox*, *Google Drive*, *TeamViewer*, *Evernote*, *Steam* and many more. You select all of the apps that you want to install and click the large Get Installer icon. It then downloads a very small program which, when run, will then scurry off and install each and every program you selected without a further key press from you. No reboots will be required during the installation process of any apps and all default installation options are taken. You see a progress bar, with details of the apps installed or installing shown underneath. No additional junk such as toolbars or other bundled software are installed – just the apps you asked for and nothing else.

What makes this really useful is that you can keep that installer and when the inevitable time comes to reinstall Windows you just run the same installer – it'll then reconnect to their servers and pull down the latest version of those very same apps you selected.

The company makes its money by offering a Pro version, charged monthly, but this is squarely aimed at IT staff having to manage larger numbers of users. It covers more apps and provides a number of other enterprise-level features.

I've lost count of the times I've used this app when restoring my (or someone else's) PC, although I tend to download a new installer each time as I always look through the list of software to see if there's anything else that's been added that I might want to install. It's such a simple idea, yet it saves so much time and also ensures that you don't inadvertently download malware-infected versions of a program or forget to install it altogether. Just run it, go make a cup of tea, come back and it's all done.

 More info: www.ninite.com

Never lose your golf balls

According to Mark Twain 'Golf is a good walk spoiled'. I personally tend to agree, but appreciate there are a lot of people out there that do indeed enjoy hitting a small sphere with a long metal stick. One of the (many) problems with golf is that if, like me, your experience and skills are somewhat limited you may spend a great deal of time hunting for lost balls or money replacing them.

Golf ball finder glasses are now a reality to pull you away from this drudgery! After putting on the glasses grass, foliage and trees will become much darker, with golf balls glowing and therefore appearing much more prominently.

It's not a problem if you already wear glasses, as they are lightweight, weighing in at around 36g and are designed to slip on top of most prescription glasses.

The makers don't recommend wearing them as sunglasses and they also don't offer any form of UV protection. I wouldn't recommend wearing them as sunglasses either if you are looking to make friends and influence people. They are supplied with a nylon carrying case that can be clipped to a golf bag or buggy.

The glasses themselves can be purchased for around £10. For about the same price you could of course buy yourself a pack of 24 golf balls. So the question you should ask yourself is 'am I a bad enough player that I am likely to lose more than 24 balls or waste a lot of time looking for the balls that I do lose in order to make this purchase worthwhile'?

While they may not look the most aesthetically pleasing things you can hang off your face they do appear to work. There are significantly more positive reviews than not, although many also state that white flowers such as pansies can deliver 'false positives'. Still, for under a tenner they make an ideal present for the golfing enthusiast in your life. If golf is a big part of your social life then I think they'd be worth a punt at this price.

 More info: www.amazon.co.uk

Remotely control your PC, tablet or phone

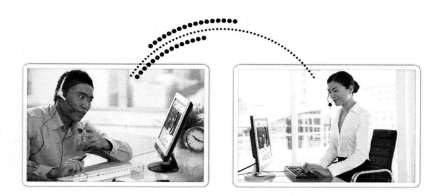

There are various reasons why you may need to remotely access a computer, tablet or phone. Maybe you're away from home and want to access files on your PC from another computer. Or perhaps you want to connect to a friend's device to show them how to do something on it.

TeamViewer is one of the most popular applications out there that offer remote control, simply because of the level of devices it supports. Let's start with the PC, Mac and Linux versions. Download and install the software, which is free for non-commercial use and you are instantly ready to remotely control another computer, allow remote control of your computer or start an online meeting. In addition to sharing screens you can also have text, audio and video conversations with the other party as well as hear sounds from the remote computer. You can even transfer files to/from each computer.

To start a remote session the software needs to be installed on both computers, each with an internet connection. The host PC will display 9 digits and a password, which the user can pass to the other person over the phone or email. They in turn enter this information in their copy of *TeamViewer* and within seconds they will be connected as if they were sitting in front of the other user's PC.

The meeting aspect of the software is more aimed at collaborative online sessions where up to 25 people can join, control and share screens. Control can be passed between users and other tools such as whiteboards allow people to quickly share ideas.

What sets *TeamViewer* apart is that the desktop versions can also take control of certain mobile devices, although iOS is limited to screenshots and certain system information due to restrictions within the software by Apple. However, you can easily connect to, say, an Android tablet or phone from a PC and use the touch screen via the mouse on your computer.

If you need to consider *TeamViewer* commercial licenses, pricing starts at around £30 per month per license, but if you think of the cost of having to jump in a car, train or plane in order to get in front of a computer then this starts to look very appealing.

As I mentioned at the start of this book, I tend to be tech support for my friends-and-family network, so the first app I recommend installing is *TeamViewer* in case I need to help them with something. Probably at least once a week I have to say to someone *'OK, double click on the TeamViewer icon and read out the nine digits. Now read out the password.'* It's so much easier than asking them to tell me what they see on screen... I recall one occasion where a friend was trying to copy music from her PC to an Android phone and needed some help. I connected my desktop PC to her laptop and my laptop to her mobile phone, both using *TeamViewer*, and it was as good as being there.

 More info: www.TeamViewer.com

Play classic video games for free

Welcome to The Official Site of MAME Development Team

If you're 'of a certain age' you'll remember when video games in the arcades cost 10% of what they do now, and you may still have a yearning for those wire-frame or pixelated games of old. Games like *PacMan*, *Star Wars*, *Defender*, *Donkey Kong* still play well today, despite being nearly four decades old.

Fortunately it's not too difficult to recapture that golden era of gaming using a very popular emulator called *MAME* (Multiple Arcade Machine Emulator). Using copies or 'ROMs' of the original arcade game *MAME* attempts to reproduce that game as faithfully as possible on modern computing hardware. *MAME* can currently emulate several thousand different classic arcade video games from the late 1970s through the modern era.

MAME is Open Source and has been in development since the late 1990s, initially for Windows but now also available on Android. It was available on iOS for a short time before Apple pulled it from the App Store.

After you've downloaded and installed the Windows version you next need to find some ROMS. These are the original game files, and they are remarkably small. Given that today's games take dozens or gigabytes, ROMs from the 1980s were generally measured in just a few kilobytes – that's literally a few thousand *characters* of code, versus today's games which are millions, if not billions. There are various websites that provide ROMs for download, but note that although many of the people or companies involved in writing the original games may not be in business any more it may not necessarily be legal to download and play these games.

Installing ROMs is not an overly-complex process, but you must follow the procedure of placing relevant files in the correctly-named folders.

Another alternative to *MAME* is playing games online via websites such as *free80sarcade.com*, which hosts online versions of many arcade games, along with games from the popular Atari 2600 console. Although they may not host some of the more obscure games they are an immediate way to get your quick nostalgic hit.

Finally, if you do want to get your retro gaming fix but don't want to jump through any of the above-mentioned hoops, try the iOS or Android app stores. Some publishing houses have released packs of retro games, which you could be playing within minutes of putting this book down!

 More info: www.MAMEdev.org and www.free80sarcade. com

Make bathtime more fun!

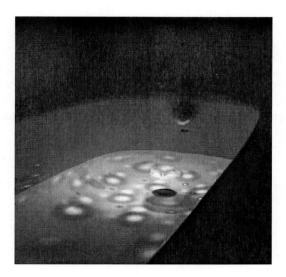

Sometimes getting the little darlings into the bath at bathtime can be, shall we say, 'problematic'. To a child a bathroom is a boring, functional place that takes them away from whatever more entertaining activity they were doing at the time. Therefore anything you can do to make it more interesting is going to make the task much easier.

Enter the underwater disco light show. This waterproof unit comes with three colourful LEDs which are powered by three AAA batteries. Choose from four different light patterns by pressing the button on the top – from soothing phasing lights through to a psychedelic party in your bath.

Each style is made up of different combinations of lights using different patterns and displays, some flashing and some still. The dome shape allows the light to illuminate the entire bathroom. A special balancing weight is also included so it can float, and the unit is 100% waterproof. As the plastic is hard they are also safe for all ages.

This could be one element of a romantic bath for two, although you'd probably want to steer clear of the more energetic light settings for that! This is of course not just limited to the bath. If you're lucky enough to also have a spa or pool then pop a couple or even a few of these in to liven up any party.

At around £8 it's a great and unusual stocking-filler and could make the difference between a stress-filled battle washing the kids or a time they look forward to. Stick it on disco mode and it might be just what you need to put you in the mood before a night out. Judging by the reviews these are used by adults and children in equal measure.

 More info: Firebox.com

Get a virtual reality headset on the cheap

Virtual reality, or VR has now officially become 'a thing', with the *Oculus Rift*, Samsung's *Gear VR* and Sony's project *Morpheus* all vying for large amounts of your cash, but there is a significantly cheaper way for you to see what all of the fuss is about.

Virtual reality works by placing a screen in front of your face with a left and right image slightly out of sync with each other to give a visual perception similar to that of your own eyes. As you move your head the video image you see moves in sync. So for example you could be in an underwater world surrounded by fish or seeing a bird's eye view as you fly over a city. The main market for the more expensive headsets is of course gaming, as they work in conjunction with controllers to allow you to interact with your virtual environment, but there are a great deal of videos that are already available in VR format, with *YouTube* having a dedicated section called *360*.

The most cost-effective headset you can buy today comes in the shape of *Google Cardboard*. It takes advantage of the ubiquitous smartphone and, as the name suggests, is effectively a cardboard housing that you can slot most phones into. Google released a specification, so there are a variety of manufacturers making slightly different versions, and you may want to check that the one you select will fit your phone. Most will work with 5"-6" handsets. Essentially for around £10 you get a sheet of pre-cut cardboard and some lenses that bring the image into focus. Note that some don't come with head straps, so check for that if you want them, as otherwise you'll have to hold the unit on your face while using it or find a creative way of keeping it adhered to your face! Once you have chosen your headset, it's just a case of downloading the app, scanning the QR code on the side (which tells the app which Cardboard-compatible headset you have) and you're good to go.

When you view a VR compatible video the app utilises the accelerometer in your smartphone to move the image as you look around. It's surprisingly effective. As an educational tool VR is excellent. You can go on field trips without leaving your room, and *Google Streetview* already works with *Cardboard* meaning that you can instantly be transported to most of the populated world in an instant. A number of artists such as Paul McCartney, Muse and U2 have even recorded gigs in *360*, which you can view on *Cardboard*. You can also create your own 3D images for viewing on *Cardboard* with your phone and an appropriate app, which will certainly add another dimension to your holiday snaps!

One of the possible down sides of VR is motion sickness, so if you are thinking of investing in one of the more expensive headsets for gaming you might want to try *Cardboard* first to see whether you are likely to be affected.

Expect to see VR in many more places as the tech becomes even more affordable. Theme parks are already combining VR with traditional roller-coasters, so imagine experiencing all of the forces that your body goes through on a roller coaster with the visual stimulation of, say, flying through a space battle!

 **More info: Google.co.uk/get/cardboard
and: YouTube.com/360**

Record videos of your PC screen

If a picture says a thousand words then video takes it to another level altogether. Have you ever tried to explain to someone how to do something on a computer, or wanted to show them something on your PC? There are times when remote desktop apps like *TeamViewer*, covered earlier, are suitable, but sometimes it's better to make a video which can be watched again and again. This is especially useful, for example, when training staff on how to use certain software or how to perform a specific task.

CamStudio is a free Open Source screen-capturing software for Windows that can record industry-standard 'AVI' format video files. Once downloaded and installed you can select to record a specific window, region or the entire screen. If you want to just record the screen without audio then it's a case of click to record, click to stop and save your file.

CamStudio does actually include a few more heavyweight features. Firstly, if you have a microphone installed you can record your own voice. You can even enable your webcam to record a 'picture in picture' video of yourself narrating over your screen-captured video. Alternatively, if you'd rather be silent and off-camera you can also overlay text annotations in sync with your content. System audio can be recorded instead if you don't need your own narrative. (If you did need both system and spoken audio then I'd recommend using video editing software to mix the sound later). For software demonstration videos you can even highlight the cursor, overlaying a transparent yellow circle outside of your mouse pointer. Videos can be recorded in AVI, MP4 or the (rapidly dying) Shockwave Flash SWF format.

What's also very useful is that there is a version of *CamStudio* for *Portableapps*, again covered earlier. This means that you can have a USB memory stick in your pocket that will allow you to quickly make a recording on someone else's computer without even having to download and install the software.

The budding YouTubers amongst you can even use *CamStudio* to record games, although you'll have to play around with the settings in order to get the best quality, and you'll also need a fairly high specification PC to play games and record video at the same time. I'd recommend reviewing *CamStudio*'s support forums to see what settings other users have had success with.

CamStudio is one of those tools that you may only use once in a while, but it's very simple to get the hang of and invaluable for quickly creating screen-captured video. You'll probably use very few of its features, but it's worth playing around with the software to understand exactly what it could do for you either now or in the future.

Note: Ensure that you download *CamStudio* from the SourceForge link below and not the developer's own website, as their version contains adware as a way to monetise downloads from their own site.

 More info: https://sourceforge.net/projects/CamStudio

Hide data from prying eyes

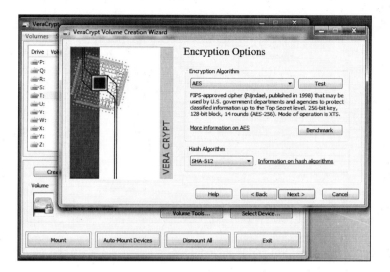

It seems like every day we hear another horror story about hacking – whether it's multinational companies losing all of our personal details or individuals who have suffered identity theft. If you are paranoid about losing sensitive data then you may want to consider data encryption. Windows has '*Bitlocker*' encryption but it's switched off by default and only included with higher versions. Mac OS includes *FileVault* disc encryption which you are prompted to enable during initial setup, and Linux also has a few options.

There are a number of encryption products available. You may have already heard of one Open Source system – *TrueCrypt* – but this suffered a series of security issues and in 2014 development ceased. Another company took up the reigns of this software, fixed the issues and continues to develop it under the name *VeraCrypt*.

VeraCrypt works by creating a 'container' file on your hard disc. It's available for Windows, MacOS and Linux. During creation you specify how much space you want to allocate to this container, which can be as large as you want, and then allocate a drive letter. You'll end up with a single file on your hard disc which will store all of your encrypted data. Each time you boot up your system you'll be prompted to 'mount' the container by entering your password, after which you can access the drive as if it were a physical hard disc, e.g. a drive 'E', for example. Any software on your computer will recognise it as such, so it is completely transparent during daily use. Just drag and drop files to the new drive as you would normally. What is actually happening is that files are encrypted 'on the fly' in memory and then written into the encrypted container file. After use you click on the unmount icon and the container is closed, instantly making all of your files inaccessible to any nefarious characters that might gain access to your computer.

Containers can also be hidden, so unless someone knows what they are looking for your data will be invisible. Also, if someone were to find the file and examine it they are constructed in such a way that it is impossible to identify it as a *VeraCrypt* file, which the developers refer to as 'plausible deniability'. Encryption is only as good as the algorithm in use, and *VeraCrypt* utilises a number of respected algorithms such as *AES*, *Serpent* and *Twofish*, all of which are encrypted to 256 bits. What this means is that it'd take a supercomputer decades to crack your password should someone wish to do so. Backing up a container is very straightforward as you only have one file to back up! Ensure that the container is closed and then just back it up to an external drive.

If you are truly paranoid about security then system encryption is the best option, which *VeraCrypt* can also take care of. This requires 'pre-boot authentication', meaning that before the Operating System loads you'll be prompted for a password. I'd recommend reading the documentation thoroughly before encrypting your entire drive, and make sure that you have a backup of everything, as if you make a mistake here or something goes awry there's no getting your data back! If you just want to secure sensitive business files or hide that collection of 'artistic photos and videos' then an encrypted container created with *VeraCrypt* is still a very secure option. Just don't forget your master password!

 More info: VeraCrypt.codeplex.com

Fault-find your Wi-Fi

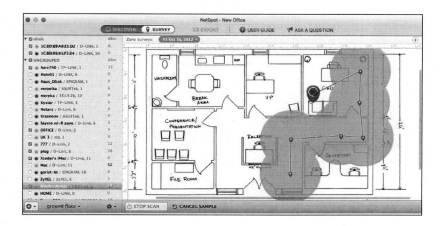

These days we all rely heavily on Wi-Fi – TVs, smartphones, tablets, laptops, games consoles and even smart fridges are all trying to get a piece of you wireless network. When problems occur it's difficult to know where to start. Is the problem down to a weak spot in the house? Are there too many Wi-Fi hotspots close by all competing for the same signal bandwidth?

Netspot Free is a product that aims to troubleshoot your Wi-Fi network by identifying its strength alongside all of the other detectable networks. Wi-Fi networks generally broadcast on a given 'channel number' – from 1 to 11. If too many networks are broadcasting on the same or near channel number then this can negatively impact on your network's performance. *Netspot* displays a live graph that changes over time, showing the channels horizontally and the strength of the Wi-Fi signal vertically. All identified Wi-Fi networks will be displayed, and you may be surprised as to just how many may be bleeding over your own.

If you've identified that your network is being crowded, changing the channel is simple. Find how to log into your wireless router's control panel, which is usually a series of numbers such as 192.168.0.1, followed by a username and password. These will either be with the original instructions or may even be printed on the back of your router. Once logged in find the dropdown option for 'Channel' and change it to the least crowded number that *Netspot* shows as least crowded – that's it. After rebooting your router it will use the new channel automatically each time and you won't have to reconfigure any of your connected devices.

Netspot also allows you to create a multi-level 'heat map' of your property. You can select one or more Wi-Fi networks, specify a rough area or load in an image of a floorplan and then take some reference points, e.g. at the corners of the floorplan. You can then use the mouse to check the signal strength at a given location and plot it on the map. Once complete it will change the colours on the map depending on the strength of the signal so you can pinpoint any weak spots. Once you've identified where your weak spots are you can then work out the best way to tackle them.

Although it's outside the remit of this book I can recommend some quick tricks to try to boost your Wi-Fi speed. Locate your router as centrally in the building as possible, and keep it away from other devices that may emit signals, such as cordless phones. Position the box high up and, wherever feasible, don't keep it in a corner. A practical, if a little unsightly option is to wrap a cereal carton in tin foil and position it behind the router to reflect the signals back into the room. If your router allows it, replace the antenna with a larger one. Also, run Ethernet cable along the skirting or under the floorboards to utilise some of the network ports – wired is always faster than wireless, and it will also free up wireless bandwidth for other devices. I'd always recommend this for desktop computers and games consoles that are invariably located in the same position all the time.

Netspot is free for both Mac and PC, with higher end paid-for versions available for commercial use. It's certainly cheaper to try to resolve issues with your existing network than either upgrading your router or investing in Wi-Fi extenders. Alternatively *Netspot* will help confirm your suspicions that your existing router is perhaps not up to the job.

 More info: www.Netspotapp.com

Turn any car into a smart car

New cars are bristling with technology these days, often including tracking capabilities, Wi-Fi, engine performance tracking and journey logging, but you can still enjoy these features even if you have a car that's a little older. Since the mid 1990s all cars have been fitted with an OBDII (On Board Diagnostics socket) generally located under the dash. These are used by mechanics to diagnose problems with your vehicle, and to provide analysis of the engine's performance.

The *Vinli* is a small device that takes advantage of the OBDII socket, pairing with your smartphone via Bluetooth. Connecting it is simple – just reach under the dash and plug it in. Next create a free account on the vin.li website in order to gain access to their app store.

The *My Vinli* app is your first port of call. This allows you to create a 4G Wi-Fi hotspot (if you subscribe to pay as you go data), setup accident detection and notification and view advanced diagnostic information about your vehicle. The Wi-Fi option will certainly keep the kids quiet, but I'd recommend you make sure that it's capped, as if you've got a couple of kids streaming *YouTube* videos for a long journey you could find yourself chewing through a large amount of data.

Once you log in with the account created earlier you can now browse and install further applications, and this is where the *Vinli* really starts to show promise. At the time of writing there are around a dozen or so applications available for iOS and Android, covering safety, entertainment, diagnostic, parking and social. *Dash* is one of the stand-out apps, reading all of the engine data and providing it in easy to understand infographics. If an engine light comes on not only will it tell you the severity it'll also give you an idea of how much it might cost to fix!

Lock & Key provides 'find my car' capabilities. If it's stolen the app will alert you, provide you with real-time tracking and alert the authorities in one click.

Home Connect stretches the connected automation further, by linking your car to your home. If you're using Samsung's *SmartThings* (covered later in the book, providing a range of switches and sensors covering motion, moisture, presence, etc.) you can create a set of rules that are enacted when certain events are triggered. For example, you could close the garage door automatically and set the thermostat to a lower temperature as you leave or turn the lights on as you arrive.

Beagle is a useful app when you're sharing the car with the kids. It will monitor their driving speed and tell you where they are. Where Big Brother really kicks in is that you can set a geographic 'ring-fence' as to how far they can travel and set other rules such as speed limits. If they break any predefined rules you are notified by SMS.

Several of the other apps listed are marked as 'coming soon' so this is clearly a work in progress. *Vinli* sells for around $200, with *PAYG* data purchased separately. At the time of writing it's only shipping in the US, but by the time you read this it (or maybe alternative products) should be available outside of the US. I believe there will be a big market to retrospectively make cars smarter, so do your research thoroughly first!

 More info: www.vin.li

Get a better alarm

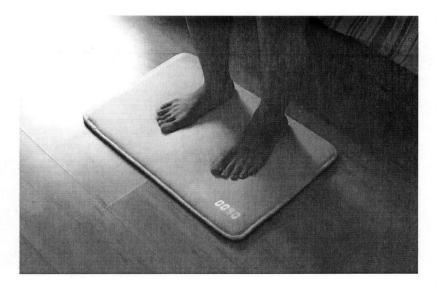

Mondays are rubbish. Getting up is never easy, especially when it's cold, dark and far too early. It's all too enticing to hit the snooze button for '10 more minutes', but this often leads to a rushed start, skipped breakfast and culminates with you joining all of the other snoozers in the inevitable traffic jam on the way to the office.

A Canadian company believes they have a solution with the *Ruggie* alarm mat. When the alarm activates there's no button to press – instead you have to stand on the mat for a minimum of three seconds, and this time can be extended if desired. The chances are that now you're up you are not going to crawl back under the duvet again.

In the top left corner of the mat is a bright LED which, when touched shows the time and also doubles as a night light, perfect for those late night trips to the bathroom. If you've got wooden or tiled floors you'll actually appreciate treading on the mat, as it's built using soft memory foam and finished in felt. No more shocks to the system first thing in the morning!

The alarm can be set using a set of five buttons hidden underneath a zip located at the top of the rug near the LED screen. You can choose from a range of soothing alarm sounds, including birdsong and running water. You can also use the USB port to connect the *Ruggie* to a PC and transfer your own 'motivational message', which will be played immediately after the alarm has been deactivated. Expect to be able to add further alarms later, perhaps with other functionality as well, as the unit's firmware can also be updated via the USB port. The *Ruggie* is powered by 3 x AAA batteries and the outer cover can also be removed for washing.

Don't worry if you have pets that take a liking to the *Ruggie*. If they sleep on it the alarm will still go off, however it may deactivate within three seconds if they remain on it. Choose a loud enough alarm and they are likely to move pretty swiftly. The built-in speakers are about the same volume as those found in a smartphone, which is around 75-85db.

Ruggie was funded on KickStarter and shipping was scheduled for September 2016 with an estimated retail price of $99. If *Ruggie* can wake you up five minutes earlier, assuming you live to 80 years old, you would have gained 100 days to your life. The makers claim that a third of people press their snooze button three times or more, so if you fall into that camp this may well be a good investment.

 More info: www.ruggie.co

Control your heating from your phone

The Internet is gradually extending its steely grip from primary devices such as PCs, mobiles, tablets and games consoles to other more mundane items in the household. The *Nest* thermostat is definitely a good application of technology for something that many of us use every day – our central heating system.

The *Nest* is a smart learning thermostat that's a replacement for your existing thermostat and works with most central heating systems. It comes in two parts – the thermostat itself and a Heat Link unit that is connected to your boiler. Professional installation is recommended.

You can either put the *Nest* in place of your existing thermostat, mount it on another wall and power it by a nearby socket, or purchase the *Nest* Stand. *Nest* is designed to be something that you want to display on your wall. Its bright LCD lights up when you walk into a room and can display the temperature or a clock in digital or analog format. What's smart about it is that as you use it *Nest* starts to learn your habits and will set the temperature accordingly.

As it's connected to your Wi-Fi network you are not restricted to controlling it at home. Perhaps a meeting got cancelled and you'll be home early – pull out your phone, open the app and you can set the heating to be nice and warm by the time you get home. It also turns itself off when you're away, saving more energy. *Nest* can also control your hot water, so you can make further savings by switching it off if you know you're not going to be using it, and if you're away during a cold spell *Nest* can even turn the heating and water on to protect against burst pipes. The app keeps a history of all of the adjustments you make and can show you how much energy you've saved. *Nest* state that in the first five years since launching in 2011 they've saved over 4 billion kWh of energy.

It doesn't stop there. *Nest* already have two other products that link to the thermostat – a smoke/CO2 detector and security camera, both of which can be controlled via apps and also talk to each other. Furthermore *Nest* has its 'Works with *Nest*' programme, and integrates with several other IoT (Internet of Things) devices, including Philips Hue lighting, Whirlpool washing machines, sprinkler systems and even pet feeders. Again, these devices will learn your habits, so for example if *Nest* knows you're away your alarm system could be activated or lights could be configured to come on/go off at specific times, or you could connect and control any connected device remotely.

In 2014 *Nest* was acquired by Google, so they now have very deep pockets. As everyone fights for a piece of the IoT pie it will be extremely important for devices to talk to each other. There are already different standards, as there already are with mobile phones with iOS and Android, so it's important to ensure that you 'back the right horse', as mentioned later on in this book.

Nest appears to be pitching itself as the hub for your connected home and already plays nicely with a reasonably wide variety of similar devices, but if it is incompatible with your existing IoT hardware then take a look at *Hive*, which is a comparable alternative. *Nest* is available for around £200 plus fitting.

 More info: www.Nest.com/uk

Get a completely free 'Office' Suite

When it comes to Office suites Microsoft has ruled the roost for literally decades, but many people balk at the idea of spending several hundred pounds for the full suite, which includes the core applications of word processor, spreadsheet, presentations, database and email/calendar. They are now pushing their *Office 365* product which is much more favourably priced, at around £6 per month for all apps, but it's still yet another subscription hitting your account each month that you could probably do without.

Open Source software comes to the rescue yet again in the shape of *Libre Office*, which is a more popular fork of another well-known suite called Open Office.

In some ways *Libre Office* is superior to *Microsoft Office*. It supports importing of many different file formats that MS Office does not, and can even run from a USB stick (see *Portableapps*.com, covered earlier). There are also some features that you'll find in *MS Office* that aren't in *Libre Office,* but there is a lot of documentation that shows the comparison between the two in detail. Chances are that they are not features you would ever use. It's worth spending time to review them all the same.

In comparison to the Microsoft 'ribbon' interface Libre's toolbar can look a little dated, but the layout is not dissimilar. All of the basic tools work as you'd expect them too, so the learning curve is certainly not steep. Libre can also open and save all Microsoft document formats.

Another strength is that where MS Office is only available for Mac or Windows, *Libre Office* runs on Mac, Windows and other operating systems such as Linux, meaning that whatever OS you run you can still have an Office suite that is common to all of them.

There are six core applications within Libre. *Writer* and *Calc* cover the word processing and spreadsheets accordingly, with Impress doing a pretty good job of mimicking *PowerPoint*. *Draw* is a desktop publishing app for designing brochures and is comparable to *MS Publisher*, while *Base* is a clone of *MS Access*. Finally *Math* provides advanced equations and formula editing, with *Charts* allowing you to embed graphs into documents, spreadsheets, presentations or drawings.

One notable exception to the suite is an alternative to *Microsoft Outlook*, but this is also well-covered with the Mozilla *Thunderbird* email client and *Lightning* calendar app, both of which are Open Source.

Libre Office has a massive online community, with many additional extensions to add functionality to each app along with templates that provide the building blocks for things like newsletters, invoices or presentations. On *YouTube* there are also a great deal of video tutorials to cover both basic and more advanced features.

Microsoft does have one more ace up its sleeve in the shape of it's free Offices apps at *live.com*. In addition to its online version of *Outlook* (spawned from *Hotmail*) it does provide free, cut down versions of *Word*, *Excel* and *PowerPoint*. They are somewhat limited, so if you do anything more than write a basic letter or add up a column of numbers in a spreadsheet you'll want to take a closer look at *Libre Office* or crack open the wallet for an *Office 365* subscription.

 More info: www.libreoffice.org

Learn any software

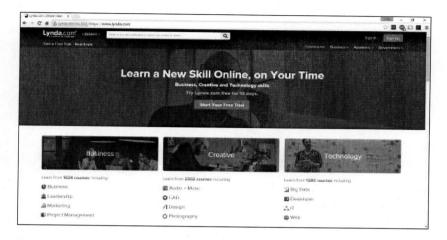

Today, if you had to learn a new piece of software your first port of call would most probably be *YouTube*. While this is fine for those 'how do I' simple questions to learn one specific function, what if you need to learn an entire application from scratch? Although there are many series of tutorials on *YouTube* they can be incomplete, of varying quality and may reflect older versions of software.

Lynda.com is a subscription website with over 4000 video courses, all of which are recorded to a consistently high quality. There are courses covering general business products such as *Microsoft Office*, graphics video and design software such as the Adobe suite (*Photoshop, InDesign, Premiere, After Effects*, etc.) through to programming languages, 3D animation, photography and music. There are even personal development courses on subjects such as communication skills.

Once you create an account you have access to a 10-day free trial, after which you subscribe, either on a monthly basis or you pay up front for a year. The latter provides the benefit that you can also download courses for offline viewing, which I can say from personal experience is very handy for plane or train journeys!

You can access *Lynda.com* videos through their website, but there are also apps for iOS, Android and Windows. The iOS and Android apps are also compatible with *Google*'s *Chromecast* HDMI dongle (which turns any TV into a smart TV). This means that you can start a video on your phone and 'cast' it to your TV, then using your phone as the remote control.

Course lengths range drastically, from some short tips-and-tricks videos running for half an hour or so to other courses spanning 10-15 hours. The courses are broken down into chapters, with each chapter containing multiple videos, all of which run for only a few minutes. This makes it very easy to dip in and out of whatever device you're on, and when you return it'll start from where you left off, marking all of the previous videos as watched. You can of course watch any videos again should you want to, and this is quite useful if you're returning to a procedure a few months after watching the videos initially.

Lynda.com is owned by the business social network LinkedIn, and once you complete the course you can share the certificate on your LinkedIn profile, showing potential employers your breadth of knowledge. Note that LinkedIn certificates are not qualifications as such – they simply demonstrate that you've watched X number of hours of video with no formal examination at the end of it.

After the free trial the subscription is around £15 per month (with no minimum period), or slightly less if you pay up front annually. There's also a Premium version which also gives you access to the demonstration files used in the video.

I decided to run through several courses for software that I regularly use, and it's surprising how many tricks I picked up that have significantly accelerated my workflow. Given that you can subscribe on a per-month basis and can cancel at any time this is a very cost-effective way to get professional training at a time and place that is convenient to you.

 More info: www.Lynda.com

Protect your credit cards from 'skimming'

Identity theft is the scourge of modern times. Roll back only a few years and pick-pocketing was the big worry when in a crowd, but today someone can potentially steal credit card data without even touching you!

Skimming is the process of extracting the electronic data stored within a credit card. This used to be performed by reading the dark magnetic strip on the rear, but information nowadays is also stored on an NFC (Near Field Communication) chip within the card and this can also be scanned using battery-powered readers that cost around a couple of hundred pounds. They are small enough to carry in a pocket and can read cards up to 15cm away. Granted, you often need the three digit code on the rear to complete online transactions but many stores and transport networks will accept payments without any further authentication.

Fortunately these skimming devices are easily thwarted with wallets that have foil or other metals embedded into them. I've always personally preferred something slimmer in my pocket, rather than a bulky traditional leather wallet with notes on one side and cards on the other, and coins rattling around elsewhere. One such wallet that delivers this is the *SECRID* wallet. They manufacture a variety of different styles, starting with the slimmest which holds up to six cards within its 8mm thick aluminium body. A button at the bottom releases the cards for easy use, and protects them completely from RFID scanners when enclosed.

If you prefer a more traditional looking wallet or need to store more cards they also offer a leather-bound book-style version that can store more cards, coins and notes when folded out. It still includes the aluminium card storage unit within the leather outer case, but remains pretty svelte at 14mm. They even offer a twin version which, at 24mm, includes two aluminium units and thus doubling your capacity.

The slim line metal versions are available in black or silver while the leather-bound versions are available in grey, light or dark brown, black or blue.

Starting at around £45 for the metal version and about £80 for the single leather wallet they are not cheap in comparison to a standard leather wallet, but they do have a certain military 'chic' about them as you eject your cards from the simple monolithic design. They take up much less room in your pocket too.

With all forms of electronic crime becoming much more prevalent it makes sense to protect yourself any way that you can. Contactless payments are quick and user-friendly, but the jury is still out as far as I am concerned on whether the benefits outweigh the risks.

 More info: www.SECRID.com/en

Turn any watch into a smart watch

The wearable tech revolution is now upon us, as hardware continues to shrink in size and grow in power. Apple took on the smart watch market back in 2015 and immediately jumped into the lead, despite various other brands such as Sony and Samsung having products available for years.

The trouble with smart watches are that they try to be too smart. A touch screen that is barely wider than your finger does not provide any level of precision, and while the marketeers try to persuade us that it'll enrich our lives further do we really need to use a 1" touch screen when we have a much more powerful device in our pockets? Many smart watches will also fight your phone for a power socket each night, as they will barely last 24 hours.

If you've already shelled out the national deficit of a small nation on a traditional watch there is an alternative solution if you still like the idea of a watch providing you with tactile feedback, notifications and health tracking. The *Trivoly* is a tiny disc just 3mm thick that slips under most watches and provides similar smart capabilities to other watches.

Starting with the basics, it syncs with your phone via Bluetooth. Once positioned correctly on the rear of the watch by lining up a marking with the 12-o'clock position you're ready to go. It has coloured LEDs that are visible from the side and also provides different patterns of vibration alert for phone calls, texts and emails along with any other notifications from major apps such as Facebook, Snapchat, Instagram, Whatsapp and many more.

There are two versions available – the *Trivoly 1* and the *Trivoli 2*, with the latter incorporating full fitness tracking including an optical heart rate sensor. The fitness aspect is well covered, as once the data is collected by your smartphone and filtered by the *Trivoly* app it can then be sent to your favourite fitness app.

The makers also state that it can be used to take selfies from up to 25 feet away – just place your phone where you want to take the photo from, tap your watch and wait for it to buzz three seconds later to confirm the shot was taken.

You can also use it to control your music from *iTunes*, *Sonos* or *Spotify*. The disc can sense where you tap the top of your watch, so tapping top or bottom controls volume while left and right skips forward or back through your playlist.

Although the *Trivoly* last longer than many smart watches expect to be reaching for that USB charging cable every 4 days or so, which of course is still nowhere near the battery life of traditional watches. You can check the app to see the current battery status at any time.

Trivoly is another successful crowd-funding story, raising over $100,000 on Kickstarter back in 2015. The *Trivoly 1* is available for around €100, with the *Trivoly 2* costing around €30 more.

 More info: www.Trivoly.com

Add a smart door lock to your door

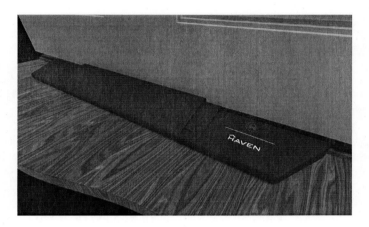

The trouble with door locks is they have one gaping security hole in that by their very design they have to be accessible from both sides. Anyone with the appropriate skills can pick it or, failing that, give the door a hefty kick. Even adding in a deadbolt is no guarantee of security, as it's more about the frame around it than the deadbolt itself.

The *Haven* smart door lock is essentially a door stop that's about the width of your door. It's securely mounted to the floor behind the door and rises when locked to create a wedge which even a battering ram cannot penetrate. It uses a rechargeable 3.7v battery along with 2 x AAA batteries for backup, connecting to your phone via Bluetooth and Wi-Fi network.

Installation literally takes a couple of minutes. While the makers suggest that some very high bond 3M tape will secure the *Haven* I think that if you're going for this level of security you'd want to do it properly and bolt it to the floor with some decent length screws.

As with any smart device it's the link to the internet that gives it its power and flexibility. It's compatible with Apple *HomeKit* and with *Nest* (covered earlier), and other safety and security devices are scheduled for development that will connect to the same network. Development to support other major home automation system brands is also planned.

You can lock or unlock the *Haven* by opening the app and one quick touch of the lock icon from any internet-connected location on the planet. If your Wi-Fi network is down *Haven* falls back to Bluetooth as a backup, and if you don't have access to your phone you can even activate or deactivate the lock via a web control panel. *Haven*'s steel and aluminium construction is encased in nylon, with all of the electronic components completely protected from the elements.

This was originally an unsuccessful project on Kickstarter, pulling in $116,000 of a $150,000 goal but the founders continued to develop the product, convinced there was a market for it and the *Haven* finally scheduled to ship Spring 2016.

The manufacturers have a compelling video on their website, showing the relative ease with which a burglar can get through a standard lock and deadbolt, but fails to get through the *Haven* secured door using full body force, a battering ram or even a sledge hammer. If security is a major concern to you then you can pick up the *Haven* lock for around $220. A separate key fob is also available for around $40.

 More info: www.Havenlock.com

Don't die from dirty water

If you're the 'outdoor' sort that enjoys long walks or camping you'll understand the frustration or even concern of being away from a clean water source for too long. Although we can live for weeks without food we can die within days without water – sooner in a hot environment. Even if water is available from a river or lake, it's teaming with all sorts of nasties that can make you sick. While most of us don't travel into such inhospitable climates it's good to know that there's tech available that can purify water from most sources.

The CamelBak *All Clear* is a 750ml water bottle with a difference. It contains a UV bulb, powered by 2 x 3.7V Lithium Ion batteries, which can purify the water from any tap or clear natural water source within 60 seconds. The UV light can kill 99.9% of all bacteria and viruses, as well as protozoa.

Using the *All Clear* is simple enough – fill it with water, screw on the cap and hold down the button for two seconds. The UV light will come on and you should then shake the bottle gently for 60 seconds until the light goes out again. The water is then ready to drink, although you should always wipe any excess water from around the thread at the top of the bottle as this may not have been treated. The cap is also compatible with CamelBak's complete range of bottles, so you can quickly purify bottle after bottle just by moving the cap.

Although neither the bulb nor batteries are replaceable the makers do stress that they should both be good for 10,000 cycles, which, if you drink three bottles a day would take you nine years. The unit is also backed by the company's 'Got your Bak' lifetime (of the product, not you) guarantee.

It's worth noting that the battery takes a considerable time to charge – five hours – but when you consider that it can purify 60 litres (or 80 cycles) that's certainly going to see you through a camping trip of a few days or more. This has been confirmed by customers, with one citing multiple uses per day over 10 weeks on a single charge.

In addition to the bottle itself CamelBak also supply a prefilter, which includes a 500 micron nylon screen to filter out sediment prior to purification. Some online reviews have suggested that this is not fine enough, but recommend backing it up with a coffee filter to get rid of finer contaminants.

The bottle is an eye-watering $99, but if you've ever been sick before as a result of drinking impure water you might be inclined to reach for that credit card. It certainly beats boiling your water or treating it with iodine.

 More info: www.camelbak.com

Safe cycling without the 'helmet hair'

Many people still choose not to wear a crash helmet when cycling. They may have a variety of reasons that they consider valid, such as the length of journey, the roads they travel down or even concerns about 'helmet hair', but the fact is that in 2014 113 people died and 3,401 were seriously injured in the UK, with three quarters of the deaths occurring because of head injuries. (Source: RoSPA).

Hövding, a company based in Sweden, has invented a cycle helmet that incorporates the airbag technology found in today's cars. In normal use the helmet is actually worn around the neck like a collar, but in the event of an accident it uses a gas canister to inflate in a fraction of a second, providing greater coverage around the front, sides and neck than a traditional helmet. The outer shell is available in a number of different styles and colour, allowing you to co-ordinate your clothing accordingly. The airbag is made of ultra-strong nylon that won't rip if scraped along the ground.

To wear the Hövding just place it around your neck and pull the zip up under your chin. There's an on/off switch on the zip tag that activates when it's attached to the right-hand side of the collar and it's turned off automatically when you unclip the on/off button. LEDs at the front show the on/off status.

The company re-enacted thousands of different types of cycle accidents using stunt riders, and also captured thousands of hours of normal cycling to come up with an algorithm that works in conjunction with the helmet's in-built gyroscopic sensors. In other words, the helmet's not likely to inflate if you sneeze or bend down to tie your shoelaces! The only type of accident where the manufacturers admit the cyclist would not be covered is the highly unlikely scenario of an object dropping on their head from above.

The *Hövding* is powered by a rechargeable battery which will give you around 9 hours of use. This is the only worrying aspect, as if you forget to charge it you could potentially be unprotected, but there are both LEDs and audible warnings, so you should have enough advance notice. Also, if you were using this for a daily commute of, say, 30 minutes, that's only 2 1/2 hours per week, giving you over three weeks of usage. As the charging socket is a standard micro-USB you probably won't be short of adaptors or places where you can top it up, and a full charge takes around 3 hours.

The *Hövding* cannot be used again once deployed and should be returned to the manufacturers, but some insurance companies may cover part of the cost of replacement. It also includes the equivalent of a 'black box' recorder, logging data about the accident that the makers say is valuable in helping them to further develop the product. Note that it is not suitable for use on motorcycles.

At £249 it's probably 10-15 times the cost of your traditional cycle helmet, but the makers are confident that it delivers a greater level of protection. Maybe it's a price worth paying if you're serious about your cycling (or your protection).

 More info: www.hovding.com

Expand your mobile phone's memory

While the memory capacities of mobile phones have increased you can still quickly eat through all of your internal storage if you are recording high resolution (1080p or even 4k) video. For example, if you record at the now standard 1080p (1920x1080) video at 30 fps it'll take 130MB per minute. That's nearly 8GB for an hour. Shooting at 4k hikes the hourly space required to a whopping 22GB!. You might think that you have no intention of recording hours of footage, but those short clips of nights out, the kids or the family pet all mount up.

For many their mobile phone is also now their daily camera, but as most have fixed amounts of memory it limits their usefulness. Help is at hand, however, in the shape of the *Leef*, available for iOS and Android devices.

The *Leef* is a small U-shaped device with a standard USB connector at one end and either an Apple Lightning or micro-USB connector at the other. It's available in 16, 32, 64, 128 and 256GB capacities and connects to your device. The iOS version, named the *iBridge*, with the main USB connector curled away out of sight around the rear. The Android version, just referred to as '*Bridge*' is smaller, rectangular and uses a sliding mechanism to make either the USB or micro-USB port available, depending on which device you are connecting to.

iOS users will also need to download an app which allows simple file transfer to and from the camera roll while also providing viewing of music, photos, videos and some document types such as Office documents or PDFs. The camera function within their app allows you to take pictures or record video directly to the *iBridge* rather than your camera roll, which you can then plug straight into a PC to either start editing or remove from the *iBridge* to free up space. Due to limitations in iOS you can't use the standard camera app to photograph or film directly to the *iBridge*.

As the Android OS allows users to access files from any app there is no requirement to download an app specifically to shift files to and from the *Bridge*, but the makers have partnered with a software vendor to provide a file management solution if you don't already have one. There are dozens of suitable apps already available that allow easy copying of files from internal to external memory cards.

The *iBridge* and *Bridge* are excellent ways of getting more out of your portable devices – be it a phone or a tablet – but there is one elephant in the room: the price. The 16GB capacity costs $59, but ramp up to the 256GB option and you're looking at just under $400!

There is a more cost-effective option though – *Leef* also offer the same design units that take removable micro-SD cards. At only $49 it's a much more attractive proposition, especially if you already own a few micro-SD cards, and gives you the option to carry multiple cards that can be swapped out in an instant.

Whether you go for the in-built memory or flexibility of the removable version the *Leef* is still a great way of extending the usefulness of a phone or tablet.

 More info: www.Leefco.com

Turn any bike into a smart, power-assisted bike

Cycling can be a very fun, relaxing mode of transport – assuming that you live in Holland where the largest incline is likely to be a curb. Many often have to rely on a bike as a main mode of transport and although your commute might be a pleasant experience if you only had to make it every so often it can become a grind when you're tired or when the weather's poor.

The *Smart Wheel* from FlyKly aims to give your legs some respite. It's a replacement rear wheel available in different sizes that fit most bikes up to 28". It contains an all-in-one Bluetooth connected unit comprising a battery and 250W motor to give you power-assisted cycling.

Installing the wheel is pretty simple. Remove your normal wheel, slide the new wheel into place, put the chain back on and tighten it up. Next, download the app for iOS or Android and then run through the configuration, providing the app with details of your bike such as the wheel circumference and number of teeth on the front and rear cogs. A handy tutorial video on these procedures will have you set up within minutes.

Once configured you are ready to use your phone to control how much assistance the wheel will provide. You can set the top boost speed up to a maximum of 16mph, a percentage for the assistance level and also a percentage for the assistance provided to braking.

Usefully, the wheel can also add an additional level of security. Just touch the padlock icon in the app and the motor locks, ensuring that if someone does hack through whatever padlock you're using they'll have to carry their ill-gotten gains away rather than ride it.

The *Smart Wheel*'s range is a respectable minimum of 25 miles, but this can potentially be significantly more as the regenerative braking system can also recharge the battery on the go. Of course, if the battery goes flat you can always peddle, so you'll never be left stranded. When you're back at base charging will take around 3 hours and the manufacturers say that the lithium battery is good for more than 1000 charges.

Available with either white or grey rims, the *Smart Wheel* works with both geared and single speed bikes. It's designed to blend in with your existing bike, and does not add excessive weight to it either, with the wheel, motor and battery weighing in at around 3kg. Note that if your bike has disc brakes you'll have to change the rear brakes to rim-based ones.

Coming in at around €1000 the *Smart Wheel* is significantly cheaper than, say, a scooter and still leaves you with the practicality and cost-effectiveness of a traditional cycle while taking some of the strain from more arduous journeys.

 More info: www.flykly.com

Be healthier at work with a convertible standing desk

We all know that sitting for lengthy periods is bad for us, but as more jobs become automated or require us to perform work on a computer many of us are now shackled to a desk throughout the working day. In addition to weight gain and the various conditions and complications that can arise from it, people often suffer from muscle stiffness and bad posture because of long periods of inactivity.

Varidesk aims to change all that with the height adjustable standing desk. It's actually an accessory for your existing desk which has a keyboard stand and slightly elevated monitor stand for up to two monitors.

When delivered it's supplied flat, but ready to use. Simply place it on your existing desk and put your monitor, keyboard and mouse back in place. When you want to stand and work just lift the monitor stand

and the unit extends upwards so that you can use your computer comfortably in a standing position. The lifting mechanism is spring-assisted and counterweighted, so you're not lifting the entire weight of the *Varidesk* and its contents.

There's an extremely wide variety of *Varidesk*s available from the basic 'Soho' range at around £150 and suitable for a laptop through to larger models priced around the £350-400 mark that will support a dual-screen monitor setup. There's even a triangular-shaped corner unit for corner desks. Most variants are available in either black or white.

Although the standard *Varidesk*s extend around 44cm, tall people are also catered for with the 'Exec' range, which extends up to 14cm higher so that everyone can find a comfortable working position.

If you're constantly dieting but never seem to reach that target weight then consider that you can burn an extra 20-50 calories per hour using the *Varidesk*, and although it's unreasonable to expect people to stand for the entirety of their working day, burning an extra 80-200 calories per day is a realistic number. While that may not sound like much, it can equate to 8-20 extra pounds burnt over the course of a year. Studies have also shown that users have improved concentration levels when standing versus sitting.

So if your new year's resolution was the usual one of 'I must lose those love handles' or you feel that your back pain is being caused through extended sitting then maybe the *Varidesk* is an investment that can help achieve that?

 More info: www.Varidesk.com

Build your own secure cloud storage

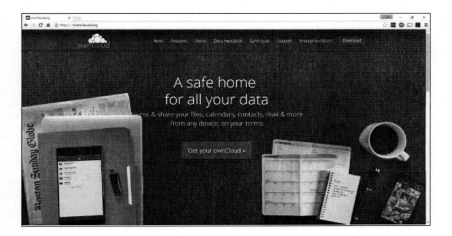

Even if you don't use it (or are even not aware of it), chances are that you already have access to 'cloud storage'. Microsoft gives you free space with Windows called *OneDrive*, Google gives you a rather generous 15GB with its *GDrive* space and Apple provides *iCloud*. There also other cloud storage providers such as *Dropbox*.

Cloud space works by effectively 'mirroring' a folder on your hard drive, copying all of its contents to a server with whichever vendor you've selected. Each time you add or save a file on your computer a small program running in the background silently saves it to their server in 'the cloud'. This is useful for several reasons. Firstly it gives you a backup in the event of your hard drive breaking or your computer being lost or stolen. Next, each provider will give you access to your files by logging into their website or using a smartphone app – handy when you're away from your computer,. You can also provide a link to share the files with others. Finally, and I find this particularly useful, if you use the same account across two PCs – say, a PC and a laptop – each one will automatically sync, keeping both computers up-to-date. The cloud space business model is based on giving you a little bit of space for free, getting you hooked and then offering more space on a monthly or annual subscription.

However, with each week bringing a new hacking story many are understandably nervous about entrusting their data to any company. *OwnCloud* is an Open Source system that can run on your own server, replicating all of the key functions of paid-for services. There may be other costs involved such as a server cost, which will be several hundred pounds a year, a domain name and a 'SSL certificate', which gives you the green padlock when you browse to the site. However, if you already run your own server you can simply set up a 'subdomain', e.g. cloud.yourdomain.com, and install it there.

OwnCloud requires the server to be able to run 'PHP' scripts (a free download) and mySQL databases (also a free download). Installation is relatively straightforward – just upload the files to your server, create an empty database and tell the *OwnCloud* installation wizard its details, and that's it. You can then create unlimited users and allocate them a specific amount of space. Next, download the client software for each PC you want to use it on. There are clients for PC, Mac and Linux, as well as mobile apps for iOS, Android and Blackberry.

Once it's set up and is running it's pretty much invisible hereafter. Each time your computer boots the client app loads in the background, giving you a small cloud icon in the tray icon list. A green tick shows that app files are updated. When you save a file you'll see the icon change within a few seconds, signifying that *OwnCloud* has identified the file as 'changed' and is syncing it with the server. If you've shared files or folders with anyone else it'll instantly be updated on their PC as well (or next time they boot up if their PC is not online).

Granted, this requires a certain level of technical expertise to install and maintain, but if you are concerned about data breaches on third-party servers then *OwnCloud* will keep *your* data with *you*. It's also a great way to securely share and collaborate with others. If you already have your own server then there's pretty much zero cost other than domain-related costs such as an SSL certificate for around £50 per year.

 More info: www.OwnCloud.org

Get online digital services starting from $5

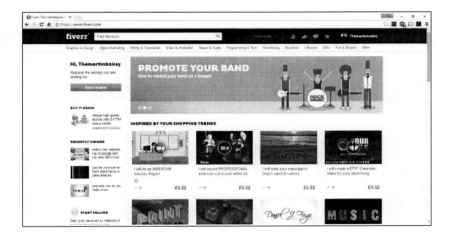

The Internet is an astounding tool for finding out anything about anything, and it's a great way to meet people that you would otherwise not come across in your offline world. It's also a great way to locate service providers that you or your business might need, and this next suggestion is definitely the ace up your sleeve when you are looking at creative resources.

Fiverr.com is a website that lets anyone publish a service, mainly relating to digital services such as graphics, design, audio/video creation/editing, programming, advertising, etc. As the name suggests, prices generally start at $5, with each seller posting a basic service (described as a 'gig') and then often offering a sliding scale of pricing for additional services. For example, you may want to hire someone to design a brochure. Type 'brochure design' into the search box and you'll be greeted with hundreds of sellers from around the world. Each one details what they will offer at the basic gig price, with additional services listed underneath. So, the basic gig might be designing a single page brochure for $5 within 3 days and providing a JPEG image, whereas additional services might include a faster service or supplying the source *Photoshop* layered image to allow you to perform further customisation yourself.

As you browse each gig you can see the seller's profile on the right hand side, along with location, languages spoken, average response time, rating and any testimonials. Click on their logo image to view their full profile along with any other gigs they may be offering – chances are that if you're interested in one of their services you may be interested in others.

Where it gets more interesting is that once you create an account to buy services from individuals on *Fiverr* you can then also immediately offer your own. It's free to join and free to list your services, although *Fiverr* will take 20% of all transactions. They also charge a small transaction fee for the buyer.

The range of categories is very extensive – from promotional services such as posting on social media about your business to some downright bizarre gigs such as 'I will act and say anything you want as a pirate for $5'.

The *Fiverr* blog also makes for interesting reading, with many sellers either posting free advice or sharing their success stories from using *Fiverr*. One seller told how he paid off his college debt and made $28,000 over four years. It's hardly a full salary, but if you can create a number of interesting and wide-ranging gigs there's a good chance that you'll be able to generate a reasonable amount of business in your spare time.

Having used *Fiverr* myself a number of times to find design and promotion services I can heartily recommend it for those looking for creative resources on a budget, or even if you want to do something a bit out of the ordinary. Even if you have design skills it's sometimes worthwhile giving one or two designers a brief to see if fresh eyes can come up with something a little different. I've employed designers to create custom graphics, this book's cover and even content for a video I made for St Valentine's day for my nearest and dearest. Take a few minutes to browse their site – I don't think you'll be disappointed!

 More info: www.fiverr.com

Build your own personalised talk radio station

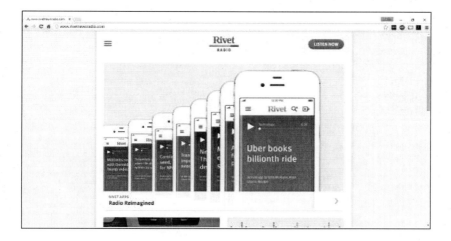

I'm a big fan of talk radio stations, especially when driving. It's good to arrive at a destination and feel that I've learnt something along the way. However, my choice of terrestrial talk radio channels is rather limited and there have been many an occasion where the topic of the hour has been less than interesting. What if you could cultivate your own talk radio station based on your interests?

Rivet Radio, available as apps for iOS, Android and via the website, is essentially a news radio station which delivers a personalised mix of news and podcasts. They pull audio files from a variety of content providers such as BBC World Service, AccuWeather, TED Radio Hour and American Public Media. There's a mix of both UK-centric news as well as stories from around the world.

After downloading the app you start by selecting your favourite categories from a list, including Government & Politics, Business, Sports, Entertainment, Technology and Lifestyle. It'll immediately create a playlist of stories that will instantly start streaming. The mobile interface is very clean, with the bare minimum of controls. Swipe to the right if you want to skip the current story, and a large Play/Pause toggle allows you to quickly stop playback if need be. A timeline shows your progress, along with time remaining. Most clips are only a minute or two long, but it's still useful to see a visual representation of where you are. Underneath the headline are three icons – Follow, Share and Save. Follow allows you to select the topic, show, host or producer, so you'll hear more from them in the future. Share allows you to post to various social media, and Save bookmarks the story so that you can quickly listen to it again later.

Although you can listen to and control the app in your car via Bluetooth, where this comes into its own for me is its integration into newer vehicle entertainment systems. *Rivet Radio* has partnered with companies such as Jaguar Land Rover and Bosch so that when your smartphone is connected to your car's entertainment system the app contents are displayed on the car's in-built touch screen rather than the phone – essentially the app is now in your car. You can use the car's controls (generally right on the steering wheel) to skip stories, and the story headline is emblazoned right across the screen.

Rivet Radio uses your mobile phone's 3G/4G connection to download content, but the audio files are heavily compressed, and the spoken word does not need to be as high quality as audio. As a result if you listened to the radio 2 hours a day, five days a week you'd probably use no more than a couple of gigabytes per month. Still, if you're on a limited data tariff you may want to run a test – clear your data usage log settings in your phone, run *Rivet Radio* for 60 seconds and then see how much data you used. Multiply by 60 to get your hourly rate.

If you have a daily commute of any length then *Rivet Radio* could leave you more informed and relaxed when you arrive at your destination.

 More info: www.rivetnewsradio.com

Play and stream any video format to any device

Over the years I've used various different devices to record video, and have also accumulated other videos in a many different formats. Sometimes I've tried to play a file and it's been missing sound, video or both. Often this is what is known as a 'codec' problem. Codec stands for Compression/Decompression and it's the algorithm by which the audio or video has been compressed. If you don't have the right codec installed the video won't play. Alternatively it may be that the default player you have installed on your system just wasn't designed to play the format you're trying to play.

The *VLC Media Player* is somewhat of an old-timer in software terms, having been around since 2001, and as a result it will play just about everything you can throw at it, including DVDs. This is useful, as in their wisdom Microsoft decided to remove (free) support of DVD playback with the first release of Windows 10.

Being Open Source, *VLC* is both free and available for multiple platforms covering Windows, MacOS, Linux, Android and iOS. It's small and lightweight, so will work well on older, slower computers, and there's no adverts or user tracking – you just get a fast, functional Media Player.

The standard interface itself is a little basic, but then again you're supposed to be looking at the content, not the player. The interface is 'skinnable' however, meaning that you can download different styles which can be applied at the click of a mouse to completely transform the look and feel.

In addition to playing all manner of formats *VLC* also handles streaming from other devices or over the internet. Furthermore, there are a variety of extensions available to further enhance *VLC*'s functionality, such as a subtitle finder and lyrics fetcher. The mobile *VLC* apps are also often better than the stock video player on your phone or tablet, again playing more file formats and having more customisation options as well.

Other developers have taken advantage of its Open Source nature to extend it's functionality even further. One such app for iOS and Android is *VLC Streamer*, which will stream movies from your library on a PC or Mac to your mobile device. Download the mobile app (of which a free trial one is available) and then download the *VLC Streamer* Helper app for your main PC. Queue up any files you want to watch and the Helper app will process them for streaming. This can take a while, but you can stream while its processing. This is great if you keep video files on a main computer with more storage capacity and want to watch them on a tablet.

VLC is truly the swiss army knife of media file playback, and third party apps such as *VLC Streamer* make it an invaluable app to install on your computer.

 More info: www.videolan.org and: www.hobbyistsoftware.com

Add a 1.5mm multi-tool to your wallet

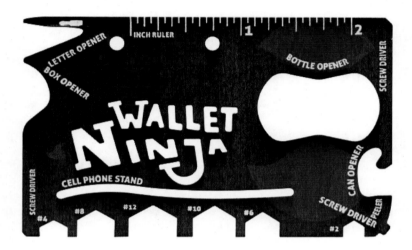

We've all had those moments where you're out and about somewhere and you just need a tool such as a screwdriver, spanner, tin opener or something similar. Maybe you're doing some DIY, crammed in a corner of the house on your hands and knees and have every tool near you bar the one you actually need. Perhaps you just like to be prepared for every situation.

The *Wallet Ninja* is ready to spring into action for any such occasion. The size of a credit card and just 1.5mm thick, it's made from steel that's been heat treated four times to make it incredibly strong. Available in either black or camouflage designs it features 18 tools cut out of various locations.

Starting with the bottom, there are six hex spanners (sizes 2, 4, 6, 8, 10 and 12), four screwdrivers (Phillips, flat head and 2 x eye glass screwdrivers), a bottle opener, a tin can opener, a letter opener, a nail puller and a box opener. Either side of the top edge is an inch and metric ruler, and the final tool is a fruit peeler. The last trick up the

Wallet Ninja's sleeve is that by placing a credit card through the long thin gap near the bottom you can also use it as a phone holder. Each tool is clearly labelled as well.

The tool comes with a lifetime guarantee that it'll never rust or bend, and reviews across several sites seem to confirm its sturdiness, which is impressive given its slim proportions.

The official website states that it fits within guidelines by official bodies (such as the TSA in America) and is safe to go through airport security as it does not actually contain any blades or sharp edges and is under 4 inches. However, there are reviews which state that some have been confiscated, but only after having successfully gone through numerous other airports beforehand. It probably depends if you get a particularly grumpy security guard. It's a shame they did not print something on it to state that it meets official guidelines as a safe carry-on, perhaps with a web address to confirm its specs. Where possible (and assuming you remember to do so) it may just be worth just slipping it to your hold luggage as you check in instead.

For around £7 the *Wallet Ninja* is a really handy tool to have in your pocket and one of those stocking-fillers at Christmas for the gadget freak who has everything. No doubt the bottle opener will come in handy over the festive season as well!

 More info: www.amazon.co.uk

Add a laser pointer to your smart phone

Having given many a presentation in my time it's often very useful to use a laser pointer, but more often than not I've forgotten to take mine with me or, worse still, the battery is flat when I go to use it in some remote location with no possibility to nip out to the shops to purchase a spare AAA.

The *iPin* attempts to save you from this tyranny of modern-day business life. Available for both iPhone and Android devices, the *iPin* slots neatly into the 3.5mm earphone jack of your smartphone. Once inserted just rotate it 90 degrees so that the small tab is not in line with the body of the phone and the red laser is activated.

If you also like to listen to music when you're not giving presentations you'll be pleased to know that the *iPin* ships with a small plastic accessory that acts as a combined extension socket and *iPin* storage unit. Just remove the *iPin* from the 3.5mm socket and plug in the accessory storage unit's own 3.5mm plug, and then plug in your earphones, with the *iPin* stored safely adjacent to it. Granted, it'll protrude from the phone about an inch more than before, but if you have cause to regularly use a laser pointer it's a minor inconvenience.

The *iPin* also ships with a very useful companion app which allows you to control a presentation via Bluetooth, Wi-Fi or using your phone's personal hotspot capability. You can then use the interface to enable or disable the laser, set an alarm, set a countdown (which may be useful if your presentation is time-limited) and most usefully you can slide left-right on the phone's screen to move between your slides.

Swipe up from the bottom-centre of the screen to enable a track pad which mimics the trackpad on a laptop, allowing you full cursor control via your phone! Short tapping once instigates a left click, while a longer single tap performs a right click. Finally, using two fingers across the screen replicates dragging. It's worth practising these controls if you have to give a presentation that requires anything more complex than moving between slides, and remember not to face the audience while using your phone with the laser turned on!

Two versions are available – the short and long version, with the latter an extra 1.8mm in length to accommodate a phone case. The laser itself is rated class II with an optical strength of under 1mW.

The *iPin* was another crowd-funding success story, achieving a 600% increase on its $10,000 funding target back in 2015. Even Apple co-founder and famous gadget geek Steve Wozniak carries one in his daily arsenal of technology. Of course, Apple are now moving away from the 3.5mm jack and some Android phone makers may now follow suit, but no doubt similar products that use a USB or Lightning socket will be developed.

Although at the time of writing there were relatively few outlets selling it in the UK, some of the US outlets are offering international shipping at reasonable rates. It's available for around US$45.00, so you're paying a premium for its size, but you'll certainly not go unnoticed in the boardroom.

 More info: www.iPinlaser.com

Get more from your smartphone's camera

In recent years the camera on the back (and indeed on the front) of your phone has improved immeasurably. Resolutions often match those of pocket camera, and flagship models can record video in 4k. But often the hardware is hampered by the camera app that ships with the phone, with the manufacturers shipping a 'one size fits all' app suitable for the masses, often missing features and manual overrides that more accomplished photographers would want to use.

For this app I'll focus on replacements for the stock iOS camera app, but there are many also for Android and Windows phones. I could easily list half a dozen apps that could have been referenced here, but my needs may differ from yours. The point here is that you're not stuck with the standard app, so hit your appropriate App Store and do some research. Many adopt the 'fremium' pricing model whereby you get the basic app for free and then unlock more advanced features.

My personal favourite for iOS is *Camera+* by Tap Tap Tap. Available in both free and paid-for versions, it packs numerous features that are simply not available in the standard camera app, so much so that you'll wonder why Apple haven't added many of them in.

Starting with the layout, the interface is clean and intuitive. The main shutter and menu icons remain fixed to the bottom of the screen, regardless of which way you rotate the phone. Above right of the shutter button is a + icon that allows you to configure the crop layout of the photos (normal, square and 16:9) along with normal, macro, timer, burst mode and *Camera+*'s stabiliser feature, which aims to avoid blurry shots by performing digital stabilisation.

Above the shutter button is an information panel showing focus, shutter speed and white balance, all of which are configurable by touching the appropriate icon and then using a slider to adjust. The screen immediately updates to show you live changes, so getting macro shots with tricky lighting conditions could not be easier. Being able to manually adjust the focus alone is a great reason to use this app. The main view itself has a 6x zoom on the right. Single touch auto-focuses and a two-fingered touch allows you to select separate focus and exposure points. *Camera+* also includes a separate Lightroom editing area, allowing you to keep general photos in the Camera Roll and only edit the ones you want.

You can enable *Camera+* to be accessible from iOS notifications, so a quick swipe down from any location including the lock screen allows you one-touch access to take a normal photo, macro shot or those ever-so-important selfies. Tether it to social media accounts such as Twitter or Facebook and you can also share straight from the app.

At around £2.30 for the iPhone version it'll cost lest than a skinny latte but puts many of the features found on digital SLR cameras right in your pocket, and may make the difference between a passable snap and a beautiful memory worth framing. The iPad *Pro* version costs around £1 more, but has more editing functions. *Camera+* may even help you to postpone upgrading if you felt that the camera in your current phone was its Achilles heel. The only downside is that this particular app doesn't support video, but you may also want to do a search to find a new video app that meets your needs.

 More info: www.camera.plus

Connect your existing camera to Wi-Fi

As this book is testament to, technology moves on at a staggering rate, and although technically speaking it does not immediately render your existing gadgets obsolete there's often the urge to replace a gadget that functions perfectly well but that lacks one or two features found on newer models. Photography is a great example of this, with compact cameras battling against today's smartphones which, as we've already seen, can give many models a run for their money.

One product that can teach an old camera new tricks is the Eye-Fi *Mobi Pro*. It's an SD memory card with a twist – it can connect to a PC, Mac, tablet or smartphone over Wi-Fi to instantly transfer your images or video wirelessly. Just replace your standard SD card with the *Mobi Pro*, available in 16GB and 32GB formats, and then install the associated app for the platform(s) you want to use it on. It's actually powered by the camera that it's plugged into, so there's no additional batteries or wires to consider.

It's a class 10 speed card, which means it's faster than the cheaper class 6's, but not as fast as some of the newer UHS cards. You can expect a 24 megapixel JPEG to transfer over in around 5 seconds. There are two connection options – direct or infrastructure. Direct mode requires you to connect your computer or mobile device wirelessly to the *Mobi Pro* as if it were a Wi-Fi hotspot. Once done it can be configured to automatically sync JPEG and/or RAW files to your device. Infrastructure mode works a little differently. Plug the card into a computer and run the software to connect it. This enables any other device on the network to connect to the card, although the card remembers the last computer on the selected network that it synced to, so if you want to start syncing to another computer you most close the app on the first one beforehand.

Many camera manufacturers have partnered with Eye-Fi and have support for the cards baked into their software. I'd recommend going to the Eye-Fi website and checking if your camera has additional support. If it doesn't, don't worry – it just means that you'll miss out on some enhancements that you might also see on the camera's menu system rather than just using the card from the associated app.

Eye-Fi also provide a cloud service whereby they'll sync unlimited files to their servers and any of your devices for a monthly fee of around US$5.

The company does offer a more cost-effective version of the card which drops the *Pro* monicker, but this lacks the finesse of its bigger brother. For example, you can't choose which files or file types to sync – it just syncs everything chronologically in order. So if you've just come back from holiday and want to grab those last shots from the airport you'll have to wait until the other 400 files have synced first.

The 16GB version will set you back around £35, with the 32GB costing around £60. Bear in mind that for this price you can buy a 128GB card that transfers (when plugged into a PC) at a much higher speed, but for on-the-go convenience the *Mobi Pro* can't be beat.

 More info: www.eyefi.com

Get a free, high powered photo editor

The de-facto standard for editing photos at a professional level is Adobe's *Photoshop*, and while they've moved to a more affordable subscription business model you're still talking about over £200 year, which just does not make sense for the occasional user.

Way back in 2004 *Paint.net* started development as an undergraduate college senior design project mentored by Microsoft, and is still being maintained by some of the alumni that originally worked on it. It was originally considered as an alternative to Microsoft *Paint*, a basic image editing package that ships with Windows, but has grown into an incredibly powerful photographic editing tool that's on a par with packages such as Adobe *Photoshop* and Corel *Paint Shop Pro*.

Packages like this differ from the likes of *Google Photos* (covered earlier) as it gives you far more control and functionality. *Google Photos* is great for tweaking brightness levels or cropping/straightening a photo, whereas with a fully-fledged image-editing package you can create complex visual effects by combining layered images or using tools to modify individual areas of an image. For example, have you ever wanted to remove something from the background of an image, such as a street lamp or telephone wires? No problem. Just use the clone tool to copy an area of sky or surrounding background over the offending area.

Start by downloading and running the installer. The interface is fairly intuitive if you've used a similar image editing tool. On the left you have a tool bar with various icons such as zoom, select, fill and crop. A history panel allows you to undo unlimited items, and the layers panel gives you a thumbnail of each layer and instant control of their order. *Paint.net* is extremely fast, so even when working with large, complex compositions only slower computers or those with limited memory will see any performance issues.

There's an impressive array of visual effects included – from blurring, sharpening, red-eye removal, distortion, noise, and embossing. You can also Rotate/Zoom in 3D, making it very easy to add perspective and tilting.

What's more useful for the beginner is that *Paint.net* has a thriving community, so there are plenty of plugins, great documentation and, on *YouTube* you can find plenty of tutorial videos to get you up and running. If this is your first foray into professional photo editing I'd recommend watching a few videos and getting comfortable with concepts such as layers and adding masks, as these are areas that new users tend to struggle with.

Paint.net is only available for the Windows platform, but there are plenty of similar (and free) options for Mac and Linux, such as *GIMP*.

 More info: www.getPaint.net

Keep biting insects at bay in the home

Do you try to avoid staying outside on a summer's evening for fear of getting eaten alive by biting beasties? Or perhaps you keep the windows tightly shut to avoid those little vampires of the night from making your skin look like bubble wrap. There's also nothing worse than turning out the bedroom light only a few minutes later to hear the high-pitched whine of a mosquito that thinks you are quietly sleeping and are now fair game.

As the threat of insect-borne diseases such as Zika become more of a concern there's a simple and relatively low-cost gadget that can help you to stay bite-free. The *Zapplight* is a low-voltage 9-watt 920-lumens bulb that also includes an even lower voltage blue LED and 1-watt bug-zapping grid. It fits into a standard screw-cap bulb socket. Turn the light on once for the normal light, turn it off and on again for both and off/on a third time just for the insect killer. This is particularly handy if you install one in the bedroom, as you can turn the main light off but still be protected overnight.

The unit unscrews to allow you to remove any dead insects, and it's supplied with a small brush to assist with scraping their charred corpses off of the grid.

The makers claim that it is effective in a 500-sq-ft room, and in a test with 20 mosquitos added to a tent it was 100% effective within minutes.

LEDs tend to last for many years, so you should have no problem getting your money's-worth out of this bulb. It's available in both US 120v and European 220/240v versions, but only with a screw cap connection so if you have a bayonet socket you'll either have to convert it or buy a low-cost adapter.

Available to buy either singularly, or in three, six and twelve packs the bulbs start at around $25 with the price dropping to around $18 when you buy the largest pack. It might be worth clubbing together with your insect-bitten friends to benefit from the bulk discount.

Speaking as someone that often returns from a holiday with a bite count in the twenties or thirties this is definitely something I'd even consider slipping in a suitcase when I travel.

Bonus tip: If you do get bitten here's a trick that really does work. Put a teaspoon into a hot drink and then tap it quickly onto the bite, holding it on there as long as you can bear. As the spoon cools you'll be able to hold it on for longer. The heat kills the bacteria close to the surface of the skin and will alleviate the itching for a while. It won't get rid of it altogether, so you'll have to do this again every few hours, but this has certainly stopped me from scratching bites. Another method is to use a hair dryer on the highest heat setting, but this is less precise than the spoon method.

 More info: www.Zapplight.com

Turn any surface into an 80" touch screen

To my mind one of the best developments in recent years that has benefitted mainstream products is the operating systems powering devices such as smartphones. More specifically, the Android OS. Being Open Source allows developers to implement it into their own products and instantly have access to a solid, stable and familiar platform that has a wide range of apps available. An excellent example of this is the *Touchjet Pond* Android-powered projector.

Over the last few years projectors have shrunk considerably, use longer-lasting LED bulbs and no longer require a fan that sounds like a light aircraft to cool a white-hot bulb. The *Touchjet Pond* was successfully funded on Indiegogo in 2015, generating over $1m. Weighing in at just over 270 grams and measuring a pocket-sized 28mm x 115mm x 100mm it has the possibility of either working as a traditional projector through the mini HDMI socket or running any Android app. It has a built in battery that's good for up to 2 hours, 16GB internal memory, micro-USB socket, 1-watt built in speaker, Wi-Fi and Bluetooth.

The unit comes with a remote control, two styluses, a charger and carry case. The remote can actually be used like a mouse but the real selling point of the *Touchjet Pond* is when using a stylus – 80" Angry Birds on the living room wall, anyone? The stylus can be used either right on the wall itself or just in the air, and as it's supplied with two that makes multi-play possible.

Setup is simple – just power it on, calibrate the touch pens on the surface you're projecting onto and then connect to the Android Play store. At 80 lumens (or 50 when running on the battery) it's not exactly bright, so you'll have to pull the blinds, but it does not need a very dark room to deliver reasonable images. Note that the bigger the image the darker it'll be, so if you need the full 80" you will need to make the room as dark as possible to get the full benefit.

This projector really does have a great deal of applications. For business users it gives you an ultra-portable device for presentations that you don't need cables for. Mount it above a desk and you've got a very cool design pad where you can draw straight on the desk and then save your work for later editing. At home it's great for gaming and movies, and if you don't have a wall to project onto, how about watching a film in bed on the ceiling? The micro-USB port (supplied with a standard USB) adaptor allows you to plug in a phone, memory stick or portable hard drive so you can view content anywhere.

The only downsides are that the resolution is not full HD, running at 854 x 480, but it's still better than DVD quality. There's no keystone correction (which allows you to adjust the pitch/angle of the picture if the projector is not pointing squarely at the wall), but otherwise it crams a hell of a lot of functionality into a very small package.

The *Touchjet Pond* is available in black or white and will set you back a shade under £600. If you don't need the touch screen functionality but like the idea of a small, lightweight and battery-powered projector there are plenty of Android-powered alternatives available at half the price, so do a little research based on the factors that are important to you. As an all-rounder the *Touchjet Pond* is difficult to beat.

 More info: www.touchjet.com/pond

Get a better workout on the treadmill

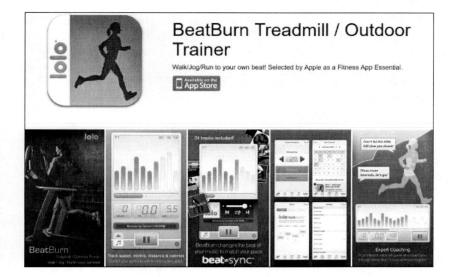

Some people get a real buzz out of running – whether it's outside or on a treadmill. For the rest of us we need all the motivation we can get, and it's proven that running to music can help you push yourself that little bit further. That's all very well, until that playlist you have set to shuffle moves from a high octane dance track to the latest tear-jerker from Adele. Fortunately salvation comes in the form of a phone app – Lolo's *Beatburn Treadmill* app for iOS.

It's essentially a replacement for the standard music app on your phone and uses what the makers call Beat-sync technology. This shifts the tempo of your music to match the pace of your feet, or as they more eloquently put it, helps you to capture the 'Saturday Night Fever strut'. It'll pick the next track based on the profile you initially create, along with your current speed, and adjust the tempo if you speed up or slow down.

Beatburn also includes its own personal trainer, providing motivation and advice to get the best out of your workout. You can increase or decrease the intensity of your workout and the trainer responds accordingly. It's a real voice rather than a computer generated one, so it doesn't feel too scripted or robotic.

As with an increasing number of apps, *Beatburn* syncs with *Apple Health* and also has *Apple Watch* support included. The app tracks and stores information such as incline, speed, distance and calories burned, displaying it on an interactive graph. If you're serious about your running/health you can also connect it to most Bluetooth heart rate monitors, and of course you can track your history and share progress on Facebook or Twitter.

Beatburn Treadmill costs £2.99 and is currently only available on iOS. It comes with 24 tracks of high energy music included in the price, which is a good deal on its own! If running's not your thing you can also check out their elliptical trainer or indoor cycling apps, as well as other apps focussing on abs, weights, food and yoga. Bundle deals on multiple apps are also available in the App Store.

If you've struggled with motivation in the gym *Beatburn* could be the difference between a mediocre workout and a great one, and for the price of a couple of doughnuts that you probably shouldn't be eating it's worth a go.

 More info: www.lolofit.com

Be safe when walking alone

As a man it's difficult for me to truly understand how a woman feels walking alone late at night, but we've all been in a less than savoury area the wrong side of midnight at some point and perhaps wished that someone was at least aware of where we were 'in case anything happened'.

Our smartphones give us access to a combination of technologies that can help – communication, audio/video recording, location awareness and 'crowd-sourcing' through your friends and family network.

bSafe is a free app for both iOS and Android that should be an essential install, if not at least for women and children then perhaps for everyone.

Once you've downloaded the software you'll be prompted to create a profile, consisting of your name , number, email and gender. Next, create your Social Safety Network of friends and family. You can add as many as you want, but they'll also have to have a *bSafe* account. Adding them will send off an invitation to them to download the app and join. You can allocate one contact as your primary contact so that in the event of an emergency they'll receive both a text and call.

The app has an impressive array of features. Firstly, Follow Me allows you to share your location via the phone's in-built GPS and, more specifically, the route you plan to take to your destination with your network in real time. Friends will be sent an invite to follow you and you'll be notified once they accept. You can set a timer so that, say, after 30 minutes they'll be notified if you've not arrived and checked into the app. Note that having the GPS switched on for any length of time will deplete your battery faster than normal, so do take that into account before you set off and ensure that you either have plenty of charge or perhaps a portable charger with you.

At the bottom of the screen is a large SOS button. Trigger that and your entire network will be notified, a siren can sound (if you've enabled it) and the phone will also start to record video and audio, which could be useful in the event of an attack. Video, voice, location and timestamp data is also stored on their servers, so in the event that the police need to be involved you have evidence stored remotely and securely.

Finally, *bSafe* includes a killer feature for those about to embark on a date – the fake call. Set a name and a time delay and your phone will emulate a real call giving you the excuse you need if you find yourself on the date from hell.

bSafe also offer a premium version, whereby they allocate someone to provide security in the even of your friends not being available, but this is currently only available in Norway and Sweden.

This has to be one of the best uses of technology, and it's a shame that manufacturers don't have an in-built solution that covers all of this from a safety aspect.

 More info: www.getbSafe.com

Get relief from snoring

There's nothing worse than still being awake in the small hours when your partner is blissfully in the land of nod making a noise like Darth Vader mating with the Tardis. Not getting enough sleep can make you feel lethargic, stressed and long-term it can be detrimental to your health. Short of surgery (or murder) there was little you could do about it – until now.

The *QuietOn* ear buds combine two technologies – noise cancelling and acoustic noise attenuation to effectively cancel out the noise around you. They're also incredibly small. They fit inside your ear but claim to provide similar noise reduction to on-ear noise cancelling headphones. The active noise cancelling uses a microphone to sample the sound around you and creates a 'phase shift' (or equally opposite sound) to cancel out the original sound. It's especially focused on reducing low frequency 'bass' noise not often addressed by normal earplugs.

In full-size on-ear noise cancelling headphones the microphone element is located outside the ear. However, in *QuietOn*, the microphone that samples the sound is located directly inside the ear canal. This allows *QuietOn* to more accurately produce anti-noise that results in good noise cancellation at the ear drum. By locating the microphone in the air volume of the ear canal, *QuietOn* is also able to reduce noise that is conducted by the skull into the ear.

Both the design and use of the ear buds is simplicity itself. The case is also the charger. Remove the buds from the case and they are already switched on, so there's no on/off switch. Insert the buds in your ear and rotate to put them into position. The built-in battery should last about 50 hours,which should get you through an entire week of constant nightly use – pretty impressive in such a small device.

Note that these are not traditional headphones in the fact that you cannot listen to music on them. You simply take them out the case, plug them in and enjoy the silence. Given their simplicity they can easily be used by children as well, perhaps helping them to concentrate when doing homework.

The charging case is also pretty small, at 59x30x22mm and weighing in at just 25g, so they won't take up much room in a travel case. The earbuds themselves weigh under 4g including the battery, and measure in at 19mm depth and 22mm in height.

Of course, their usage is not limited to drowning out snoring. They're great for filtering out aircraft noise or even just if you want to tune out the hustle and bustle of your office or home.

The *QuietOn* ear buds were funded on Indiegogo in early 2016, blasting through their target of $50,000 by over 800%. You can pick up a pair for around €160.

 More info: www.QuietOn.com

Transfer old videos and cassettes to digital formats

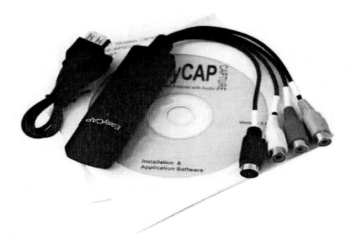

Technology is great for the here and now but as it moves forward it often leaves legacy formats in its wake. VHS and audio cassettes have now reached that stage, with most of us no longer reserving space in our living rooms for devices that have lived there since the early 80s. In a few years we may be having the same discussion about DVDs. So what do you do with all of your tapes languishing in a drawer that you can no longer use? There are plenty of companies that for a small fee will transfer the contents of a VHS cassette either to DVD or will provide you with an MP4 file on a USB stick. Alternatively, and for probably a similar price of a single cassette transfer you can do it yourself! This logic also applies to vinyl and music cassette tapes,

I'm not recommending any specific brand here, as most of the advertised products will be unbranded. If you search for VHS to USB on any popular auction site you'll find a multitude of products that will do the same job and most of them will cost around £7. Do take a moment to check if the unit supports your operating system, especially if you are on a newer Windows system or running Mac OS – most of these low cost systems will be Windows-only. Once you've reviewed what's on offer and selected your product from a reputable buyer place your order and get your old VHS or cassette player out of the loft in anticipation of the delivery. Connecting this up will be very simple. One end will have a standard USB port which you connect to your PC and the other will have the white, red and yellow phono sockets. These should connect to relevant sockets on the rear of your player – an audio system will have just white/red, but VHS will use the yellow for video. Some VHS players don't have the phono sockets, so you may have to invest in a SCART cable with phono sockets at one end or a SCART to phono converter.

Most of these devices will be supplied with a CD that will contain two things – drivers and software. It may also contain a PDF manual if no paper manual was supplied, so take time to look. When you connect the USB it'll instantly try to find drivers online. That may well work. Alternatively just use your file manager software to run the setup program from the CD. Once complete there will most probably be a new icon on your desktop, which will be the device's own software. This is usually in the form of a Media Player style app. If you've connected your player up correctly you may even be able to press Play and the video/audio content will already start playing on your PC. After this it's a simple case of clicking the on-screen record button to start creating your file.

I would recommend recording a one-minute test before transferring anything of significant length. Firstly, quite often the recording settings are set to a low resolution. A quick peek into the settings might show a dropdown or toggle switch that allows you to make a better quality recording. Secondly, especially for video, if you record for one minute exactly then you can take a look at the file size and work out approximately how much hard disc space it will consume. Bear in mind that if you've got 20 tapes, with each one being 3 hours long and each minute was 10MB (and it could be considerably more – this is just for easy calculation), you're going to need 36GB of space!

For the price this is a great way to ensure that those memories of yesteryear don't degrade or get lost over time.

 More info: www.ebay.co.uk

Remotely check on and entertain your pet

Did you ever wonder what your pet gets up to when you leave the house? Worse still, maybe you are already acutely aware of their capabilities after coming home to the devastation that a bored pet can wreak. Owning a pet comes with responsibilities, but with full-time jobs and perhaps a long commute that can limit the time you have to spend with them.

The *Pet Cube* is a 4-inch cube that allows you to remotely see, communicate and play with your pet when you're away from home. It connects to your Wi-Fi network and communicates with either an Android or iOS app on your phone. On the front of the *Pet Cube* is a 138 degree camera, which streams video at 720p resolution. It also includes a speaker and microphone, allowing for two way communication between you and your feline or pooch.

The real trick up it's cubed sleeve however, is the 5mW 3R class laser, which can be controlled remotely via the mobile app. If you've ever watched a cat or dog play with a laser pointer you'll know that it's a great way to entertain both them and you – imagine not only being able to confuse Tiddles or Fido by invisibly talking to them but also driving them crazy with a laser from any internet-accessible location on the planet. The makers also suggest that you can help to keep your pet fitter by the regular exercise they can get.

The base of the *Pet Cube* is covered in rubber to give it grip (I assume in case your pet tries to pull it off the table) but it also takes a standard tripod mount, so you can position it safely out of harm's way if need be.

One aspect of the *Pet Cube* that I find slightly creepy is that you can share access to your device. That's fine for friends and family, but the makers also offer the ability to share access across the entire *Pet Cube* network. I'm not sure how I'd feel about coming home to find some stranger screaming abuse at my pet, but thankfully you have the option of disabling sound. Having said that, you can disable audio for shared *Pet Cubes*, and of all of the pets I looked at while researching this none had sound enabled. Even so, it's not uncommon to connect to a *Pet Cube* and feel like a fly on the wall as you watch the owners of their house go about their daily lives.

You can pick up the *Pet Cube* for around $199. If you want to get more of a feel for the *Pet Cube* why not download the app for free and freak out someone else's pet today!

 More info: www.petcube.com

Get free Design/Desktop Publishing (DTP) software

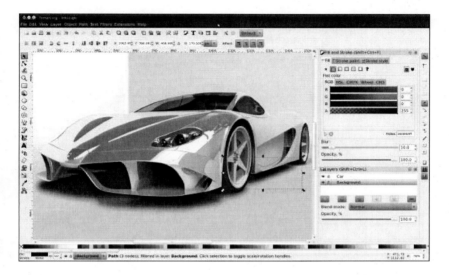

Roll back 20 years or so and vector-based design or Desktop Publishing software used to be limited to high end publishing houses. With the advent of the PC and products such as Adobe *Illustrator* and *CorelDraw* the barrier to entry was reduced to only a couple of hundred pounds. Open Source removes that barrier now altogether in the form of *InkScape*.

Although the image above shows a sports car drawn purely by hand using vector graphics, *InkScape* can be used for a variety of different projects, such as creating logos, designing a brochure for print or laying out the basic design structure of a website.

Start by downloading the Windows, Mac or Linux version to your computer and then run the installer. The interface is similar to other vector graphic tools, with toolbars left and above the main work area, with dockable information panels.

Starting with 'object creation' you have tools to quickly create shapes such as circles, rectangles, stars/polygons, or you can draw freehand, also with calligraphy-style strokes. Once you've drawn a shape you can manipulate it by editing points (or 'nodes') within your newly created shape. You can have different fills and strokes (outlines), as well as different levels of transparency, meaning that you can drop a logo over, say, an image rather than just having it on a plain background.

One of the more advanced features is called 'Bitmap tracing', whereby you can convert a picture into a vector-based image. This can be used for things like cleaning up a scanned logo or converting an image to something where you have a specific editing requirement that you could not do in image editing software. Text handling is well supported. In addition to being able to create 'boxes' of text you can fit text along a path or inside a shape.

It also handles advanced vector functions such as interpolation. Let's say you want to create an image of a square merging to a circle over 10 steps. Interpolation would take the square and circle and create 8 steps in between where the square gradually morphs into a circle.

Once you've created your masterpiece you can export it in a variety of formats, including the Open Source SVG format, PNG, DXF or Adobe Acrobat PDF.

InkScape is extremely well supported and documented with plenty of online manuals and video tutorials to get you started. There are also various forums and free downloadable templates, ready for you to drop your own content into. If you have a flair for design or simply need a more creative design tool than standard 'Office' products can provide it's worth a download.

 More info: www.InkScape.org

Attach a smarter lock to your suitcase

As someone that travels regularly for business I can attest to the fact that 'jetsetting' is actually a pretty joyless experience, moving from one airport queue to another, with that niggling fear that when you arrive at your destination you'll be minus your luggage, or that anyone with access along its journey will have had a quick rifle through to relieve it of anything of value. Placing any old padlock on your case is not necessarily the solution, as unless it's approved by bodies such as the TSA it'll simply be cut off.

The *AirBolt* is a Bluetooth-enabled smart lock that does not require a key or combination, instead talking to your smartphone to unlock. An app for both iOS and Android will unlock it with a single push of a button as long as you are the owner and your smart phone is within range of the *AirBolt*. To prevent accidental unlocking it will simply re-lock itself if the rope is not taken out of the locking mechanism.

You can set alerts so that if you are parted from your case you're notified on your phone as well as via a buzzer built into the bolt –

useful if you've ever absentmindedly walked away from your case in a shop or airport lounge.

The big potential problem with such a device is 'what if the battery dies'? The included Li-ion battery uses the low-powered Bluetooth 4 protocol, so it should be good for around a year, but you can top it up easily via micro-USB if necessary. If your phone should go flat while you are on your travels you can download the app to a friend's phone, log in and unlock it. Alternatively you can set up a unique backup code using a specific button combination on the lock itself.

As with the *Tile* tag covered earlier in this book the *AirBolt* also takes advantage of crowdsourcing to locate your bag should you be unfortunate enough to lose it. The makers also state that they intend to not just rely on other *AirBolt* users, but plan to tap into other smart device manufacturers that utilise crowdsourcing. This is excellent, as it means that if, for example, your bag is lost at an airport and you log into the app to report it, there's a high chance that it will pass by either an *AirBolt* or similar user, whose phone will then alert the network of its location.

The *AirBolt* is TSA-approved, which I guess means that the makers have given them a backdoor to unlock the device rather than cutting it off. You can attach one to your suitcase for around £40.

 More info: www.theAirBolt.com

Better bike storage

The average family of four is likely to have one car, possibly two, along with bikes for at least the kids and maybe the parents as well. Storing the bikes can be a significant problem, also taking up valuable space. Worse still, if they're just left outside it creates more work to keep them cleaned and maintained, with the probability that they'll rust as well.

The Italian-built *Flat Bike Lift* is a ceiling-mounted hydro-pneumatic overhead bike rack which can be used either in a garage or within the home to easily store your bike horizontally against the ceiling.

Once mounted to your ceiling you start by pulling on the bar to lower the mechanism. The wheel rest height is around 67cm in a standard 2.4m garage, so you need to be able to lift your bike enough to rest the wheels into the U-shaped wheel groove. Sliding the bike forward places the saddle into a locking mechanism, and there's even a space for your helmet to be stowed. Then you just apply a minimal amount of lift to push the bike towards the ceiling as the gas spring takes the strain. There are four different positions that you can calibrate the unit to – 10, 14, 18 or 22kg, based on the weight of your bike. For the more mechanically-minded readers the radius required by the *Flat Bike Lift* as you raise it is 145cm. This is important as it may have a bearing on where you mount it if you want to place/retrieve your bike when a car is already in the garage.

Once the bike is parked you can easily still park a car underneath it, as the unit sits just 45cm away from the ceiling (excluding your handlebars) – just remember that if little Johnny wants to go out you may have to move your car before he can get to his bike, depending on the size of your garage.

There's also options to add a second bike, get longer length handles (for taller ceilings), heavier duty gas springs and custom mounts for unusual-sized bikes.

There are other similar products available, but the *Flat Bike Lift*'s inclusion of hydro-pneumatic springs makes this a very easy product to use, especially for children or those without enough upper body strength to lift a bike onto a traditional wall-mounted bike rack. It's a great way to reclaim space in your garage or to maximise storage space elsewhere within the home. Its customisable design also lets you tailor it to meet your needs. You can pick one up for around £180.

 More info: www.flat-bike-lift.com

Communicate with and track your dog

If you've watched the film *Up* you may recall a rather talkative dog called Dug that used a collar to communicate in plain English. While this next gadget doesn't stretch that far it does go a considerable way to bridging the communication gap between you and your four-legged friend, as well as keeping an eye on their well-being and location at the same time.

The *Kyon Tracker* collar includes an impressive array of sensors in a device weighing just 60g. It uses low-powered Bluetooth 4.0 to communicate with an app on your phone, but also includes an LED display on the collar itself to show messages. The GPS and altimeter work together to not only tell you where your dog is, but also at what height to within 10cm – useful if he's run up to the third floor. Heat and water sensors tell you if your dog is too hot, cold, or has perhaps got into trouble in water. An accelerometer, GSM and an ultrasound buzzer are also included.

The *Kyon* is also supplied with a base station. As well as charging the collar's 30-day battery it creates a 300ft perimeter. If your dog strays out of range you are immediately notified of it's location via the GPS tracker and using the collar's in-built GSM. The LEDs will also flash up 'I AM LOST', along with your mobile number so that you can be quickly contacted. The same ring-fencing trick can be applied using your smartphone as a 'base' when you're out and about.

The 9-axis accelerometer is used to track the dog's motion over time, alerting you if there is irregular activity. The buzzer can emit a high frequency sound designed to calm your dog if they get into a stressful situation, such as a confrontation with another dog. The same ultra-sound module can also be used quite effectively to stop a dog from barking.

The makers claim that it includes an emotion sensor which can display your dog's mood, whether it's feeling sick and the collar can even remind you to give any required medication or to walk your dog! You can also customise the collar to display your dog's name.

It's available in a variety of colours, small, medium and large collars from 25cm to 50cm and can take a leash force of over 30kg. The *Kyon Tracker* will set you back around $250 for the collar and base station along with a monthly fee of $4.99 to cover the GSM data costs. While this ongoing cost might seem like yet another monthly drain on your bank balance I guess this really depends on whether your dog is the type that frequently runs off or is often in danger of fights with other dogs. What I like most about the *Kyon* is how the manufacturers have combined a wide range of sensor technologies to provide an all-in-one single solution.

 More info: www.Kyontracker.com

Turn fire into electricity when camping

If camping's your thing then you'll know that there's nothing better than cooking your own food on a camping stove in the middle of nowhere, far from civilisation. Camping has its compromises though, one of which being that you're a long way from a power outlet.

The *Biolite* camping stove aims to plug that gap. It's a wood-burning stove that has a thermoelectric generator on the side which converts heat into electricity. This powers a fan to help generate a hotter flame which the makers claim is not only similar in temperature to gas-powered burners but also a cleaner, more efficient burn with less smoke.

Using the *Biolite* is simple. Fill the chamber with any form of biomass such as twigs, pinecones or wood pellets, set it on fire and wait. Note that there's no in-built lighting mechanism, so you'll need matches. You shouldn't have to wait too long once your fire is started before you have a usable heat, with the honeycomb heat mesh letting in plenty of air and the fan directing it. You can set the fan speed between low and high temperature, ranging from 3.4kW to 5.5kW. In real terms that means that you should be able to boil 1 litre of water in about 4 1/2 minutes with around 46 grams of wood.

Underneath the power switch is a USB port which can generate 2 watts of electricity. For the average mobile phone this equates to about 60 minutes of talk time from 20 minutes of charging time.

The company manufactures a range of similar and accompanying products, such as the 'kettle pot' and portable grill, both of which attach to the *Biolite* to extend its functionality. They also offer various lights including the FlexLight that has a gooseneck cable and grid of LEDs providing 100 lumens of light via the USB port of the *Biolite*.

Many seasoned travellers seem to agree that this product works well in the field, with the reviews largely positive. The main caveat seems to be that the wood needs to be very dry, but the same could be said of any wood-based fire. As the chamber is relatively small you'll also need to ensure that you regularly feed it with fresh wood.

It must be very satisfying to be in the back of beyond, cooking your dinner and then plugging in your phone and hearing that familiar charging notification. You can pick up the *Biolite* camp stove for around £125. A smaller version is available for around £90 and the larger BaseCamp model with an integral grill, 5W electrical output and side fuel entry to easily keep the flames stoked.

 More info: www.Bioliteenergy.com

Improve your golf swing

If you play a sport for fun, practice can help you improve over time, but sometimes you need that little extra help to take your game to another level. You could hire a coach but this can be costly and you may have to work around their schedule.

Zepp has become something of a leader in the field of sports trackers and now offer trackers for baseball, tennis, softball and golf. We're going to focus on the last offering. The *Golf Swing Analyser* is a small yellow puck that connects via a mount to your golf glove, with both left and right handed users supported. It connects via Bluetooth to either iOS or Android phones and uses a 3-axis gyroscope and two accelerometers to track your swing in full 360 degrees.

Start by pushing one corner of the sensor in to power it up and then plug it into the glove mount on your glove. You have to calibrate the sensor to the club you're using, but this only takes a few seconds so does not really get in the way of your game.

Once you start swinging the app immediately reports back information such as club speed, club and hand plane, tempo, backswing and if your phone is in your back pocket it'll even log your hip rotation.

The killer feature is that you can compare your meagre attempts with the pros using side by side video playbacks, so you can see exactly where you're going wrong and what you need to do in order to correct it. Each of the previously mentioned measured statistics has its own screen and when the app notices a trend it'll prompt you to watch a specific video to help you improve. These videos are also available through the Zepp website if you prefer to watch them on a larger screen.

After you've taken 30 swings the Zepp will crunch 90,000 data points and produce a detailed report on what's good, bad or indifferent about your game, providing tips on how to improve. Many reviewers suggest the tempo and swing measurements have helped them to improve the most.

The Zepp *Golf Swing Analyser* is available for around £85 and is supplied with a USB charging cable (but no charger – you'll have to plug it into any USB port) and glove mount. The battery lasts for around 8 hours with a 2 1/2 hour recharge time and the on-board memory can log 2000 swings. It weighs in at just 8g, so you'll hardly notice it on your glove.

The free app does provide you with some features before you decide if you want to purchase the *Zepp*, such as the tutorial videos and the ability to record and compare your swing with the pros, so it costs nothing to get a few free tips under your belt before you hit the fairway.

 More info: www.Zepp.com

Get discounts in stores and online

This is more of a train of thought rather than a recommendation of a specific app or website. Whenever you are shopping for anything higher value than groceries you should always consider what options you may have to buy it cheaper.

First off are shopping scanning apps. Have you ever been in a store and wondered whether the special in front of you could still be purchased cheaper, either at other retail stores or online? *RedLaser* and *ShopSavvy* are two apps, available on iOS and Android that both offer scanning of standard 'vertical line' UPC bar codes as well as the square 'QR' codes. Fire up the app and scan the bar code. Within a few seconds they will scan various online merchants and/or local retailers, providing you with a table of vendors and prices. If the store you're in has a price-match guarantee then you only need to show your phone at the checkout to get the discount. I've done this successfully a few times. The quality of local results can vary between the product and/or the app itself, so download and try a few to see what works for you. Scanning a product bar code in store is certainly quicker than manually typing a product code into Google on your phone and then trying to sift through the results while you're being eyed up by the sales staff that know precisely what you're doing!

Next, when you're going through the checkout process of any major online store look out for the coupon or voucher code field. This should be like a red rag to a bull, and the next question to cross your mind should be 'where can I get a code to fill this lonely looking box?'. Online stores often offer promotions that are limited by criteria such as geography, or perhaps they've provided a discount code for a limited time or to a specific company. People often like to share this little nugget of knowledge, so before you complete the checkout process open up a new web browser tab and type in the name of the store followed by 'voucher codes'. The first hits in Google will be sites such as *vouchercodes.co.uk*, *myvouchercodes.co.uk* and *hotdeals.com*. Another hot tip – hold down the CTRL key (on Windows, Command on Mac) and click on the first three or four links. This will open these sites up in new browser tabs one after the other, so while you're reviewing the first site the others are silently loading in the background. Granted, this can be a little hit-and-miss – some vouchers may have expired or not be valid for local stores, but it's worth spending a couple of minutes sifting through the first few results on Google to see if you can strike it lucky.

One area where I've personally had a great deal of success is with any brand of pizza firm. In fact I'd go as far as to say that I've not paid full price for a delivered pizza for literally years. Just find a relevant code and enter it during checkout. There's normally a 'validate' button to the right of the code field, so you can see right away if the discount will be applied or not. If not, try another code – it costs nothing to try.

Finally, it's worth signing up to discount voucher sites such as *Wowcher* or *Groupon*, as you'll get notifications in your in-box of items you are interested in.

I've probably saved a four figure sum or more over the years using tips like this, and these are only scratching the surface. Add in price comparison sites and the price you pay for virtually anything you buy becomes negotiable.

A stylish, eco-friendly way to keep cool

Being British, I'm used to moaning about the weather. Despite our summers often being humid (as well as wet) many of us do not feel the necessity to invest in energy-guzzling air conditioning in the home, so we suffer in silence when the mercury rises. Desk fans only offer momentary respite from the heat, with the benefit immediately gone when you switch it off.

Geizeer aims to offer a personal and elegant solution in the form of its cube-shaped ice cooler. Made out of wood, which has excellent thermal characteristics, the interior contains a fan and a specially shaped tapered gel ice pack. The 144mm cube is actually two halves, held together with magnets. Take off the top half and place the ice pack (which you will obviously have to keep stored in your freezer beforehand) inside. You can also place 'diffusers' (e.g. fragranced granules, perfume etc.) into a dedicated space at the top of the ice pack, turning the unit into an air freshener as well.

There's not even a power switch - the electrical contacts are located in two of the corners, so switching it on is as simple as rotating the top half of the cube 90 degrees, and rotating it again when you want to switch it off.

In tests a 12 square metre room can be cooled by around 3 degrees, with the gel ice pack lasting for around 4 hours before it needs re-freezing.

The Li-Po battery lasts around 6 hours and is charged via micro-USB cable, the connector for which conveniently includes an LED which turns red to show when it's charging and blue when fully charged. Having no power cable constantly attached also makes it easy to move it from room to room.

Air conditioning units are not only expensive to install and run but also can be noisy, making it difficult for some people to sleep. They are sometimes responsible for health issues such as headaches and respiratory problems. This makes the Geizeer an attractive proposition, being near-silent in operation, costing less than a penny a day to run and without any of the potential side-effects.

The Geizeer is priced at around £95, with extra ice packs costing around £13. It's available in a range of colours and finishes, with two different grid patterns in the top providing the airflow. What's unique about it is that at first glance you would not be able to guess what it does, and it would not look out of place in most office or home environments.

 More info: www.geizeer.it

Turn your home into a Smart Home

Although we've already covered a number of devices that will singularly make one aspect of your home smarter there are a number of kits that combine various sensors that can be viewed and controlled through a smartphone. This is a rapidly evolving market, with vendors fighting to pull you into their own ecosystems. Apple has *HomeKit*, Google has *Brillo* and Samsung offers *SmartThings*. While makers claim to have cross-compatibility you may find that some devices just don't work with all platforms. I've selected *SmartThings* as it works with Android, Apple and Windows phones and there are many supported devices and industry-standard protocols such as Z-Wave or Zigbee.

You start by purchasing a kit comprising of a hub, motion sensor, power outlet, presence sensor and multi-sensor, which can sense temperature, vibration and whether doors/windows have been left open. You can also purchase various other *SmartThings* add-ons, such as door handle/locks, security cameras, alarms and flood sensors.

The hub uses a standard USB power connector, and also includes 4 x AA batteries which are good for up to 10 hours should the power fail. However, note that if the power is out then your wireless router will be offline as well, therefore disconnecting all devices from the Internet, which sort of defeats the object. One possible solution is an uninterruptable power supply (UPS).

The concept behind all home automation systems such as *SmartThings* is that each device no longer works independently. For example, the power outlet offers more than just remotely switching devices on or off. It can be configured to act on events, e.g. if either the presence or multi-sensor detect someone in the room it could power up a lamp, or switch off the iron when you leave the room.

When you set up each sensor within the app you can give it a custom name and associate it with each room in your house, so you get 'plain English' messages about what has been triggered. Where things start to get really smart is when you configure 'routines' within the app. For example, you could configure a 'geofence' so that the hub knows when you're arriving home and can automatically perform specific tasks, such as turning the heating or lights on. As multiple users can be configured you can also get notifications when other family members arrive or leave. You can create one-click icons to instantly activate or deactivate multiple devices, such as in the morning or night.

SmartThings also already plays nicely with many other devices from leading manufacturers such as Bose, Philips, Sonos, D-Link and Yale, but at the time of writing does not work directly with the *Nest* thermostat, covered earlier. This is why it's important to scope out what you want from a smart home and then find which kits will work with any existing hardware you may have. The more adventurous can use the free 'If This Then That' (IFTTT) online service to create chains of instructions, such as logging motions detected in an online Google spreadsheet or if it's raining then turn on the outside lights. The starter kit will cost around £200, but expect to easily double that if you want to monitor all of your rooms and control multiple devices. Kits such as *SmartThings* are a great way to bring automation and security under one umbrella.

 More info: www.SmartThings.com/uk/

A new way to cook eggs

Eggs – we've been eating them for thousands of years, for breakfast, lunch and dinner. Whether boiled, fried or poached they're an excellent source of protein and also great for those dieting, with the average egg providing around 155 calories. As eggs are such a staple part of our diet it's no wonder we try to find ever more ingenious ways to prepare and serve them.

The *Rollie* Egg Cooker aims to provide a novel twist on the omelette. It's essentially an open-top cylindrical cooker that's not just suitable for cooking eggs.

The unit itself is a space-saving 9cm wide and 25cm tall. Even while cooking the sides are cool to the touch, making it ideal for the smaller kitchen and safe when children are around.

Start by plugging the unit in. There are no switches – just a red power light, with a green light that comes on when the *Rollie* is at the right temperature. Lubricate the inner cylinder with a little cooking spray and then break and pour in a couple of eggs. Add in a skewer to aid removal and that's it. Now you just have to wait a couple of minutes. When the eggs are ready they will have the texture of an omelette and (along with the skewer) will magically rise about an inch or so out of the cylinder as pressure builds beneath.

If you compare the cooking time to, say, boiling an egg it's significantly quicker, and the unit is easier to clean than a frying pan. It's supplied with a cleaning utensil that looks like a cross between a toilet brush and a chimney sweep. The makers also suggest that it's healthier than the traditional method of cooking an omelette using a frying pan, as you're not adding butter.

You're not limited to just frying an egg on a stick though. The manual includes around 20 recipes, not all of which include eggs! There are also various videos on *YouTube* from both the manufacturers and the general public. For example, you can create mini tortilla wraps or even Danish pastries. Slice them up and you've got a party platter of canapés fully prepared.

The *Rollie* is available for around £25. I can see this being especially attractive for students – it provides quick, cheap, easy-to-prepare food that's nutritious, and from a small, relatively low-cost device that takes seconds to clean. It's also great for busy parents that want to give their children a quick and healthy breakfast that isn't 'boring'. Genius.

 More info: www.getRollie.com or amazon.co.uk

Download furniture designs or get them made for you

If you're planning to work from home or perhaps setting up an office then before you start working at all you'll be looking at the furniture you will need. Granted, there are plenty of places where you can buy desks, chairs and storage suitable for either home or office,but if you're looking for something a little different as well as being more sustainable, or even if you have the skills and equipment to build something yourself then you should take a look at the *Opendesk* project.

Based in London and set up in 2014 after a successful crowd-funding campaign, *Opendesk* brands itself as 'a global platform for local making'. The idea is simple – designers can upload templates of furniture that can be downloaded in the industry-standard DXF CAD file format and manufactured locally using CNC routing technology. Designers have the choice to make the license Open Source, chargeable or without any license restrictions at all. You can order items online and *Opendesk* will pass this to a local member of their network of fabricators. This cuts out the middle man, minimises the product's overall carbon footprint and helps local businesses. What this also means is that if you have access to CNC routing equipment you can download most designs for free and manufacture them yourself with only the cost of the materials to cover. Where this idea wins hands down over traditional furniture retailers is that you have the ability to customise the designs, although the level of customisation may differ depending on the manufacturer that *Opendesk* connects you to. However, you have the option to download the templates yourself and pass them to your own local manufacturer. This is great if you need a particular product to be modified to fit a specific space, want a different material or finish, or if you want to customise the furniture to have your logo engraved on it.

The range of furniture is small but growing, with nearly 20 designers and several ranges of matching products. Although the designs tend to have a similar and simple rudimentary charm they do include cable management, so are practical enough. *Opendesk* also offers access to a team that will design your complete office workspace, covering tables, chairs and storage. Pricing to kit out an entire office is highlighted on their website, with a cost per head calculated between £300 to £600 depending on the level of customisation required. With companies such as Greenpeace using *Opendesk* to kit out their North London offices it is testament to the design of the products and ethos of the company.

Delivery takes between 1-4 weeks, with all items being supplied flatpacked for self-assembly. The downloadable designs also include a PDF assembly manual very similar to any other flatpack furniture you may have purchased, with step-by-step photos taking you through the assembly process.

In general the prices are around the market average, with the option of birch plywood or white laminate finishes. For example, a one-person 'Studio' desk which includes cable management will set you back around £500, with more basic designs starting around £330. A bedside table is available for £210.

Opendesk is an excellent way of harnessing the power of the Internet to share ideas globally but manufacture them locally, supporting designers, local manufacturers and being greener in the process.

 More info: www.Opendesk.cc

Charge your phone on your bike with pedal power

If you use a bike regularly, either for your daily commute or for pleasure there's a good chance you may already have a mobile phone mount on the handle bars. This allows you to use the GPS for navigation or sports apps to track your performance. The problem is that mobile phone batteries are lacklustre at the best of times, and having the screen permanently on with the GPS also powered up will suck the life out of your battery quicker than a vampire in a bloodbank.

The succinctly named Tigra Sport *BikeCharge* Dynamo resolves this problem by harnessing the energy generated as you peddle to charge an in-built battery. This can then be used to power your phone, reaching a full charge in around 2-3 hours when peddling at around 12mph, based on a 26" wheel.

The *BikeCharge* can be mounted on most bikes, requiring 8mm clearance between the fork and the spokes on either the front or rear wheel. An alternative kit is available for bikes with larger hub diameters of between 10 and 15mm, but the manufacturers offer a complete refund should it not fit your bike.

Fitting the *BikeCharge* should only take a few minutes. Undo the nuts on the wheel that you want to fit it to, and then slide the *BikeCharge* between the fork and hub on the right hand side of the bike. (Note that it cannot be fitted to the left). Replace the nuts and then fit the 'clutch' to one of the spokes, which will turn the dynamo as you peddle. There's also a handle-bar mounted remote switch to turn on/off the included weatherproof front (white) and rear (red) lights and to view the in-built 1100mAh battery status. It has a standard USB 2.0 port which outputs 5v at 500mA – while this is not a massive amount of power compared to the average phone charger that pumps out 1A or more it's enough to make the difference between the battery percentage going up rather than down, or at least remaining constant.

The lights can be adjusted for multiple angles and lo-beam, hi-beam, or blinking modes. It weighs in at just 500g, which is significantly lighter than other dynamo systems on the market.

Users report no noticeable drag when using the device, and the reviews are largely positive. Some have reported the unit to be noisy, although the manufacturers suggest that the unit may require minor fitting adjustments.

You can add power to your bike for around £85, so this is significantly more expensive than a battery that you could have in your pocket, but for shear convenience plus the added safety of the built in lights it's a worthy addition to any regularly used bicycle.

 More info: www.amazon.co.uk

Create stunning 3D images and animations

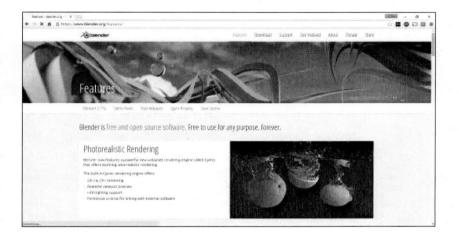

Until recently creating photo-realistic rendered images or videos was the province of high-end design studios and requiring industrial levels of computing horse-power. With processing power virtually doubling every couple of years, any current gaming PC will be more than enough to run such software, but with products such as *Autodesk Maya* costing several thousand pounds those that may want to dabble in 3D have a high price entry barrier.

Again from the Open Source fold comes *Blender 3D*, initially released over 20 years ago way back in 1995. It's free and available for Windows, Mac, Linux and FreeBSD. Before I move on I will start with a warning: *Blender* has a very steep learning curve. Be prepared to invest time to go through the hours of tutorials in order to get up and running. With that said, you're looking at a professional grade tool, and any such product will require considerable dedication to use it effectively.

Blender allows you to create complex 3D objects on a stage, position a camera and create lighting which affects all of the objects on a stage. For example, you could design a room full of furniture and characters, place a lamp on a table and the light from the lamp would light, reflect and cast shadows across any items within range. Create an outdoor scene, blur objects in the background and then add haze and lens flare from the sun. What I've described is just a single frame. Now consider that you can animate this into a scene, and then create multiple scenes to create your own movie. Note that each frame has to be rendered and, depending on your hardware, this can take a while – ranging from seconds to minutes, depending on the complexity of the scene. If each frame takes, say 30 seconds and you're making a one-minute clip at 24 frames per second it's going to take about 12 hours to render that one minute of video!

It would be pointless to list all of the features of *Blender,* as functions such as substrate scattering auto-normalizing behaviour will mean nothing to the uninitiated, and there would not be enough room anyway. Instead, if you want to explore what *Blender* can do there are a series of Open Movie Projects (read: free short animations) that showcase its significant capabilities. Arguably the most impressive is *Tears of Steel*. The twelve-minute film tells the story of a group of warriors and scientists who gather to stage a crucial event from the past in a desperate attempt to rescue the world from destructive robots. Not only is this an impressive animation in its own right but it intertwines animation with live action video – watch out for the girl flexing her bionic arm! For each open movie all of the footage, scenes and models are also available to download, so you can view the finished product and then play around with elements from the movies.

A recently available animation alternative is *Toonz*. Previously this was only available commercially, costing up to $10,000, but in March 2016 an Open Source version of this highly respected 2D animation software was released. If *Blender* is not quite what you're looking for you may want to consider this instead, although English documentation was rather scant at its release. Either way it's simply amazing what can be achieved on relatively low-cost computer hardware if you have the time and inclination to learn the software.

 **More info: www.Blender.org
or opentoonz.github.io/e/**

Camp safely anywhere

We've already covered a few products to make life in the great outdoors more pleasant during the day, but what about at night? Camping normally involves struggling with tent poles, searching for a flat surface and ultimately suffering a poor night's sleep.

The idea for the Tentsile tents was formed when the creator was six years old and saw the Ewoks in 'Return of the Jedi' living in trees. The tents are essentially hammocks using three anchor points to suspend them off the ground, allowing you to pitch up above rocks, wet ground and other areas that would normally be inhospitable to the average camper. If the conditions allow you can also use it on the ground as a traditional tent, so if you can't find three trees around you can still pitch up. You also have the added benefit of being away from insects and anything else that you don't want to get too personal with. For those travelling in environments where the wildlife can pose a threat e.g. snakes etc. this could be the main selling point.

The company has several sizes, suitable for either two or four people with a maximum weight of just under 400kg. They're also lightweight, with the heaviest weighing 9kg and packing down to 35cm x 35cm x 35cm.

Setting the tent up shouldn't take more than about 10 minutes. Start by connecting the three heavy-duty straps around your selected trees using the ratchets. There's no danger of the straps snapping if you're packing a few extra pounds as they have a maximum breaking strength of 2.5 tonnes. Next, connect the other end to each of the three tent corner eyelets and then pump the ratchets until each strap is tight, taking care to do them in intervals to get an even tension. The tent poles are broken down into short lengths but have an inner cord connecting them all together so you don't waste time trying to work out how to pack/unpack them – you just pull them out of their storage bag, find the first one and slide the next connected pole into it and so forth. Once completed, slide the two full length tensioning poles into the sleeves that cross over the top of the tent. Finally, fix the flysheet over the top and you're done. Entry is either through a front entrance or through a hole in the floor.

If you're travelling in a larger group it's useful to know that the tents are modular, so you could connect three together, make them multi-storey and even install a storage hammock underneath to keep your stuff dry and use as a step up. The Tentsile range removes many of the problems that camping often brings, and the website is worth a look to see the beautiful and often downright scary places that people have pitched their tents. Hint: some have a long drop! Prices range from around £260 for their entry level 'Flite' up to around £490 for the flagship 'Stingray'. Being a company focusing on nature they also promise to plant three trees for each tent sold.

 More info: www.tentsile.com

Become a DJ

With vinyl making somewhat of a resurgence, the idea of mixing tracks is gaining appeal again, but gone are the days where you'd have to lug around a mixing deck and a couple of boxes of records. The advent of the MP3 has allowed us to store a lifetime of music on a PC or even just a mobile phone or memory stick. However, cueing up a playlist in your chosen Media Player is a rather sterile affair and lacks any level of finesse when it comes to mixing. If you pine for the ability to cue up a track, watch the vinyl label spinning or for some scratching then the Open Source *Mixxx* software is for you!

You can download *Mixxx* for Windows, Mac and Linux. Once installed you'll be prompted to select the folder that contains all of your music. After it's scanned that it'll also scan for cover art, showing thumbnails of your track covers and even rotating them on the 'record decks'.

The *Mixxx* interface is laid out like a professional DJ rig. You can configure it with either two or four turntables. Tracks can be dragged and dropped into each deck, and from there you have a wide range of features. For example, you can quickly create a 'beatloop', automatically looping through the selected number of beats, which is useful for extending one track while you mix in another. You can change the key, tempo and pitch, and as you can see the pitch of the next track to play, you can set it before you mix it in.

If your DJ-ing skills are less than perfect you might want to fall back on the *AutoDJ* feature. Simple add a list of tracks, click on *AutoDJ* and *Mixxx* will just plough through your playlist, fading each new track in while fading out the previous one. It can instantly sync the tempo of up to four tracks so that they'll mix seamlessly together. It also plays nicely with *iTunes* as well, so you can create your playlists there first and then access them in *Mixxx*. Four sampler decks allow you to drop in snippets of audio such as jingles over tracks.

As ever there are loads of tutorials on *YouTube* to get you started and while the interface may look overly complicated at first, it's pretty intuitive to get to grips with. You only need to learn a small subset of controls in order to perform some pretty impressive DJ moves.

Mixxx has a respectable professional following, with many having input to the development of the product. There are plenty of more advanced features, such as built-in effects (flange, reverb, echo) which can be assigned to specific on-screen knobs. A master equalizer allows you to tailor the sound further to fit the acoustics of your equipment or room. There's support for many popular hardware DJ controllers, MIDI support, quad microphone support, recording of your mixes, live broadcasting over the Internet and much more.

If you've got a family event approaching and you want to do it on a budget all you need is a laptop, a good set of speakers, a stack of MP3s and *Mixxx*. You could prepare your playlist in advance but easily purchase and add tracks straight into your set on the day! Of course, nothing comes close to a good DJ, who will also have all the party tracks you've never bought, professional hardware and the skills to match, but for just creating your own mixes it's a whole lot of fun.

As an alternative, if you want to go even lighter and mix on a tablet take a look at the *Djay* range from Algoriddim, which provides a touch-based interface for iOS and Android starting at around £4.

 More info: www.Mixxx.org or www.algoriddim.com

Protect against fire without the risk of water damage

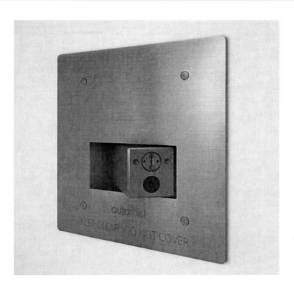

Fire can be a killer, with an estimated 300,000 domestic fires each year, of which over half start in the kitchen. While you can install a sprinkler system the damage that water can do can fall not far short of the fire it was protecting you against in the first place.

UK-based *Plumis* have developed a range of mist-based fire extinguishers, the most innovative of which is the *Automist*. The system can be retrofitted to an existing room and comprises of a ceiling-mounted detector which, once triggered, pumps water to an innocuous-looking wall-mounted nozzle. This quickly fills the room with a dense fog of water mist that removes heat and displaces oxygen from the region, starving the fire. While this may not extinguish all fires it certainly contains them, reducing damage and buying you precious time to extinguish the fire using other methods such as a traditional extinguisher.

Going back to the wall-mounted nozzle, this is mounted between 1.2m and 1.3m from the ground, is motorised and will direct the nozzle to point in the direction of the fire as identified by the ceiling sensor. The range is a pretty impressive 6m, so if mounted on a central wall it gives you 12mx6m arc of coverage. It also activates much quicker than many traditional sprinklers, with a video on their website showing Automist starting a full two minutes quicker.

The key feature is that it uses 90% less water than a traditional system due to the mist and directional spray, rather than just switching on all sprinklers within a given room. The result is less fire damage and a massive reduction of water damage to the surrounding area.

Although the *Automist* needs to be fitted by a qualified installer, the makers claim that it would cost around a third of the cost of fitting a traditional sprinkler system to a room, but also concede that *Automist* would be more expensive if you had to kit out an entire house.

The company also offers other designs, including a self-contained pump and tank unit that can be hidden behind a radiator cover, or tap units with the mist heads built in. It's suitable for all areas of the home, with various case studies detailing existing installations, along with a great deal of information on adherence to building regulations.

The *Automist* has won a plethora of awards, including the James Dyson award back in 2009 and Red Dot's Best of the Best in 2016. If fire safety or the possible resulting water damage is a concern then the *Automist* offers a practical and elegant solution that could save your property as well as your life.

 More info: www.Plumis.co.uk

Brush up on your academic subjects

Earlier we covered *Lynda.com*, which focuses on offering online learning for most of today's popular software packages. *Khan Academy* is based on the same premise of video learning but concentrates on more academic subjects.

Created in 2006 by Salmon Khan, the site aims to provide free education for anyone in the world. Khan had the idea for the site after first teaching his cousin mathematics. When other family members asked for similar help he decided to distribute videos via *YouTube*, which then led on to the more comprehensive academy that exists today.

The site may have started with mathematics but it is now host to all major academic subjects including biology, physics, chemistry, electrical engineering, economics, arts and humanities, and computer science/programming. It also contains a variety of partner content from the likes of The British Museum, Tate, NASA and The Aspen Institute, to name but a few.

When you first visit the site you are prompted to sign up as a student, teacher or parent, either using your own email address or via Google or Facebook. You don't actually need to sign up to access any of the content, so you are free to take a look at any course before you do so, but it's necessary to register in order to track your progress.. You can also assign coaches (which could also be your parents), who can view your progress and offer assistance if necessary. As users progress through each section they earn points and badges. Time online is also tracked, so parents/coaches can see whether students are using the system effectively if no progress is detected.

Courses are not limited to just videos, with many offering interactive sections to engage users further. Underneath each topic students can ask further questions, with the answers visible to everyone. A number of test exams are also available, although many of these are related to US examination standards. Regardless, knowledge is knowledge, and the ability to test yourself on what you've learned is useful nonetheless.

Although the US slant can be seen across the site – you won't find mention of the UK GCSE qualification, for example – various case studies cite success stories in countries around the world. In total *Khan Academy* claims to have around 40 million users, with 5000 courses, many of which are available in over 36 languages proving its worth as a global learning resource.

The site's slogan cites that 'you can learn anything' and that it's 'for free, for everyone, forever'. It's backed by a not-for-profit organisation with 80 employees and survives on donations rather than bombarding you with advertising. Heavyweights such as Google are among its sponsors. *Khan Academy* is not and does not claim to be a replacement for a traditional school-based education, but it can be used as an excellent supplement for a child who is struggling or for adults who need to top up their knowledge on a particular subject.

 More info: www.khanacademy.org

Change your mood (without drink or drugs)

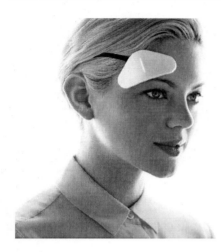

Tense, nervous headache? Is your lifestyle hectic? Do you need to focus for sport or an exam? Or do you just need to unwind? If you often have to turn to coffee, energy drinks or pills to help you concentrate, or a glass of wine to unwind then tech is once more at hand to protect your body from these impurities while enhancing your mental state.

Thync is a wearable that allows you to change your mental state in a matter of minutes, either feeling more calm or energised exactly when you need it. The device couples with any iOS device over Bluetooth to deliver neurosignals to the brain, inducing effects similar to either a shot of espresso or a glass of wine. These can last between 30 minutes and an hour, with knock-on benefits lasting for several more.

Thync's patented technology relies on low levels of pulsed electrical energy, referred to as vibes, to signal specific neural pathways, allowing users to increase or decrease their stress responses and energy levels. Start by sticking the *Thync* unit onto one of two types of adhesive strips – calming or energising, depending on the state you are aiming to achieve. This is then placed on your head, with one containing the *Thync* device on your forehead and the other in a different location depending on the strip type. The location of the strips is paramount to the effectiveness of the *Thync* and there's a tutorial video included in the app to ensure you get the right position. Next set the strength of the 'vibe' you've chosen via the app and then let it do its thing. You'll feel a slight tingling sensation in the area around the pads, but it's not painful although may be a little uncomfortable at first on the highest setting for the uninitiated.

Many have confirmed that the device does indeed help them to concentrate, relax or even sleep, and the science behind it is backed up by decades of research by the likes of Harvard, Stanford, MIT and Arizona University. Scientific studies have proven that using it daily for 10 minutes over the course of a week lowers stress, improves sleep, and raises overall mood without using any drinks or pills.

If you're worried about possible side-effects of interfering with your brain you can take comfort in the fact that the FDA exempt the *Thync* from medical device regulations due to its low power output. That being said, there is a significant list of warnings tucked away on their website. Epileptics, pregnant women and those with pacemakers need not apply, so do take a moment to read the health recommendations to see if anything is relevant.

The initial purchase will set you back just shy of $200, but the strips do make the ongoing cost add up, with a pack of five of either type costing $20, although you do get five of each to start with. The manufacturers suggest that the strips are single-use only, but many reviewers cite that they can get several uses from each strip, sometimes up to a dozen if they ensure that their skin is clean before they adhere the strips.

The *Thync* is an exciting glimpse of the future as we learn more about our minds, how they work and ultimately how to enhance them. If you currently rely on any form of substance abuse such as caffeine or stronger, then *Thync* may be a healthier, more effective solution.

 More info: www.Thync.com

Build and maintain your own website

If you need a website you have several options. You can hire a web designer to write something from scratch, which will get you exactly what you want at a price. Most web hosting companies offer online tools to help you build a site, but these tend to be limited in functionality and often only allow you to display static pages of text rather than including features such as being able to sell products online. Or you can use one of the many free Open Source Content Management Systems (CMS) that are essentially 'a website to build a website'.

A CMS will provide you with a back end administration control panel for creating pages and linking them together. Editing pages is similar to using a word processor, so it's very easy to add or amend content. Two stand head and shoulders above the rest – *WordPress* and *Joomla! WordPress* is much more popular, powering over a quarter of all websites, while *Joomla!* covers around 2.7%. However, each meets slightly different needs. Both systems require you to rent web space that can run PHP scripts and connect to mySQL databases, and this will generally set you back around £120 per year. They are optimised for search engines and are also mobile-friendly.

Each system works by the PHP-based pages talking to the mySQL database, rather than each page being written and then uploaded as a physical static document. This makes for a much richer user experience.

There's not enough space here to cover the installation process in detail, but in summary once you have purchased a hosting package you download your chosen CMS, transfer the files to your web space, create an empty database and then run through the wizard-based setup routine. Some hosts such as Heart Internet (heartinternet.uk) actually give you a one-click install for both *WordPress* and *Joomla!*, so do your research before you purchase a package.

Building a site using either system after the basic installation does have a bit of a learning curve, but again there are plenty of tutorial videos to get you started. As a big fan of *Joomla!* I've also written two books on it as well! The idea of a Content Management System is to allow you to structure as much or as little content as you want. You can create multiple categories and subcategories, storing any number of pages underneath. So you could have one on Products, another containing Press Releases and another one as a Blog. Your menu structure could link to a single page or a category, with the category either showing just the titles of the pages in a table or a snippet of the story with a link to read more, similar to most news web sites.

What really makes these systems so powerful is the vast array of extensions that you can easily install to extend their functionality. Directories, forums, shopping carts, auction systems, calendars and photo galleries are just some of the components that can enhance your site, with many of these free or at low cost.

WordPress tends to be used for simpler sites that don't require too much additional functionality and has a shorter learning curve than *Joomla!* It has many high name brands using it, such as *The New York Times* and *Disney*. *Joomla!* tends to be used for sites that need greater functionality. Both have a thriving community and can easily be 're-skinned' as required. If you need a web site and want to maintain it yourself going forward then either system will provide an excellent backbone to build on with room to grow in the future.

 **More info: www.joomla.org
and: www.WordPress.org**

Get fit with a compact, portable smart gym

As someone that has worked from home for a number of years I know the importance of being disciplined when it comes to fitness, but on those cold winter nights it's difficult to motivate yourself to leave the confines of a warm home and make the trek to the gym. The other issue is often space – few people have a spare room that they can dedicate to bulky gym equipment.

Move It is a smart home-gym system that includes four separate training equipment items – an ab wheel, skipping rope, pushup stand and resistance band which are all stored on a portable stand unit. All four items take advantage of the unit's 'smart handles'. The two handles have in-built sensors covering gyroscopic movement, pressure, radio frequency and infrared. They each include built in batteries and use Bluetooth to connect to an app on your iOS or Android phone. Simply slot the handles onto the equipment you want to use by pressing the button at the end and it's ready to use.

Each piece of equipment can detect different types of movements and your performance is logged in real time on the app. For example, the skipping rope can detect forward and reverse skipping as well as criss-cross skipping. The resistance band is the smartest of the four, detecting seven unique exercises. LEDs at the end of the handles keep you informed of its status without having to check the app.

As ever, it's the app that makes *Move It* smart. It includes a series of training programs which show your progress by counting reps and tracking calories. It also has a social aspect by allowing you to challenge friends who use *Move It*, or you can even find a 'workout buddy' anywhere in the world, which might be just what you need to get motivated if you have no-one to train with. Training progress is stored in the cloud and you can review and compare your performance over time. You can even share pictures via the app, although I suspect after a heavy workout you'd probably be more inclined to pay someone not to share them!

The batteries should last for a week and a half of training and are charged with a standard micro-USB cable, and all of the pieces store neatly onto the supplied stand with the skipping rope and resistance band wrapping around the outside handle. The unit is available in either black or white.

The *Move It* sprinted through its $30,000 crowd-funding target on Indiegogo on its first day without breaking a sweat, with shipping scheduled for August 2016. The makers suggest that you only need a 3mx3m area to work out, and *Move It* is pretty small, measuring 40x38x21cm and weighing in at a lean 3kg.

If you lack motivation, space, gym buddies or all of the above then *Move It* could be the solution that helps you to shake off those love handles.

 More info: www.move-it.club

Appendix A – Gadgets of the Rich & Famous

For the majority of this book I've focused on gadgets aimed at the mainstream, to solve the day-to-day problems that we normal people encounter. But what about those with far more 'disposable income'? Everyone knows that you can pick up a diamond-studded iPhone but there are plenty of other high-end gadgets out there whose makers will gladly relieve you of large sums of cash. Here are a few you might consider if your lottery numbers come up.

The Martin Jetpack

Alas, not invented by me, the *Martin Jetpack* actually hails from New Zealand. It can take a payload of around 120kg and has a range of up to 50km. Top speed is around 74kph and it can reach around 3000ft. It's aimed at search-and-rescue operations but no doubt you'll see the odd Russian oligarch using it to  get from their super-yacht to the golf course. Should the twin engines fail there's a built in parachute that instantly deploys, making your landing on terra firma much gentler than it would otherwise be. The Dubai government have already equipped their firefighters with a fleet of jetpacks but at $200,000 don't expect to see them whizzing around your neighbourhood any time soon.

The Groundfridge

If you want to live with as low a carbon footprint as possible you can now invest in the *Groundfridge*. This self-contained unit looks like a large bulb with a set of steps leading into it. The idea is that you bury it in your garden, leaving just the entrance hatch showing, and it takes advantage of nature's insulating effect within the ground to keep all of the food inside at around 10 degrees Celsius, which the manufacturers say is ideal for storing fruit, vegetable, wine and cheese. As it's a sealed unit it's also safe from insects and rodents, but at around €7,500 you'd have to be pretty committed to the green movement to invest in one.

The Kohler Numi Toilet

To make 'the smallest room' more of a talking point you may want to consider the *Numi* from Kohler. The lid rises as you enter the room and if it detects specific motion at floor level (e.g. men's feet) it raises the heated seat as well. Warm air flows from the base of the unit to keep your feet warm while you're seated, and the basin itself includes an air dryer, bidet 'wand' and deodoriser. A rear illuminated panel will direct you to the toilet in the dark and can be programmed to dynamically cycle through random colours, display a colour for each day of the week or show a fixed colour. It includes a touch screen remote that is charged and stored on a magnetic docking station on the wall. Beautiful, and over $6,000. I'd recommend visiting their website though at kohler.com/numi, as the photos suggest the toilet should really be a 'feature' of your main living space rather than hidden away.

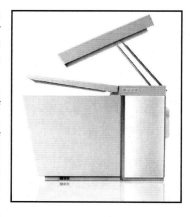

Ideum Duet Smart Table

The *Duet* is essentially a very large touch screen encased into a coffee table. It can dual boot very quickly to either Windows or Android. Available in either 42" or 46" versions, the *Duet* takes multi-touch to a whole new level, sporting up to 60 simultaneous touch points for Windows and 12 for Android. It's constructed using aircraft-grade aluminium and steel and is water-resistant to IP54. The tabletop itself is just 64mm thick with a very small bezel around the outer edges. On the hardware side there's either an Intel Core i5 or i7 processor for the Windows portion and a separate 2GHz Rockchip processor to run Android. Switching between the two can be done either through software or a physical button. Moving from one OS to the other takes around two seconds. The *Duet* is no doubt something that many of us would like in our living rooms, but with a starting price of nearly $8,000 and with hardware specs going quickly out of fashion this gadget is only really suitable for those with deep pockets.

The Smart Fridge

Intelligent fridges have actually been around since 2000 but have not really taken the market by storm. Recently several new models have launched, with the most notable from Samsung. Their Wi-Fi enabled *Family Hub* refrigerator includes a 21.5" vertical touch screen, three built-in cameras to view what's in your fridge remotely via your mobile, and the ability to share family calendars, photos and notes from any connected mobile device directly to the fridge's screen. No more sticky notes! Of course, you can also stream music, mirror video content from any Samsung TV and even re-order food right from the fridge to save you from actually having to leave the house. It'll set you back $5,000, which is enough to make anyone lose their appetite, and it also leaves less room for your fridge magnets.

The Personal Submarine

When you're not whizzing around in your jetpack you might want to explore the oceans with the personal submarine. It'll take two people down to a depth of around 300m at a top speed of 3 knots. The batteries will deliver around 6 hours of continuous fun and the unit is yours for the princely sum of $2m. For that price you also receive comprehensive training.

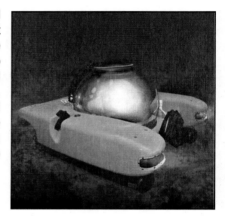

Yourself as a diamond

It doesn't matter how many zeros are at the end of your bank balance, none of us can cheat death, but now there is a way that you can immortalise yourself. Various companies offer to take your cremated remains (or a lock of your hair) and compress it using nearly 1m psi to create a diamond that is molecularly identical to those found in nature. The diamonds are available either as traditional colourless or in a variety of colours such as blue, red, green and yellow with prices starting at around £2,000 for a .1 carat size to over £22,000 for 1.5 carat. They'll also create a diamond from your pet too. But be warned – there are also reports of several fraudulent companies that claim to offer such services but may send you a stone that's never been near any human remains, let alone been made from them.

The 'Luminous Sky Portal'

If you find mirrors just plain dull then invest in the *Luminous Sky Portal*. This mirror creates 3D luminous clouds that waft around your reflection. The 80 frames of HD video create unique cloud formations and the LED back lights create beams from behind the clouds. A 36" x 24" portal will set you back $4,000.

The Robotic Bartender

After a hard day counting your millions you will have worked up quite a thirst. Why not let the *Robotic Bartender* mix you a drink from its database of 600 cocktails. The touch screen interface allows users to select from drinks such as martinis, or you can customise them by adding or omitting ingredients. The unit can hold up to 16 bottles of alcohol and 12 mixers such as cola, tonic water, etc. It's yours for $25,000.

The Flying Hovercraft

When you absolutely positively need to combine watersports with air travel then the flying hovercraft is for you. Capable of gliding over land and water, the 130hp twin cylinder engine can take you into the air at up to 70 mph and a height of 20 feet. It has a 160 mile range and can take two people up to a maximum combined weight of around 135kg. Yours for a mere $190,000.

The Lake Trampoline

If having a lake within the grounds of your mansion is not enough you can of course add a trampoline in the middle of it. It's unique design removes the need for those dangerous steel frames, and as it's made from the same 1000 denier polyester and UV-treated PVC found in military boats there should be no danger of it deflating or being punctured. It includes a ladder, high-speed motor for inflation/deflation and a secure anchor-connection kit. Unlimited lake-side fun for just $3,700.

Wear a bit of moon on your wrist

If a Breitling or Omega watch are simply just too, well, cheap for your tastes then you could invest in the *"Lunar Watch"*. Crafted from olivine basalt collected from the surface of the moon by a Soviet mission in 1974, the rock is estimated to be around 4.5 billion years old. Don't expect to get a smart watch embedded within the

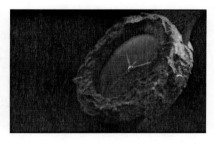

41mm moon rock, but do expect to pay $27,500, assuming you can actually get your hands on one – only 25 will ever be made.

Appendix B – Gadgets that didn't quite make it

For every must-have gadget that sells by the container-load there are many that, for whatever reason, didn't make the grade. With the advent of crowd-funding sites it seems that not a week goes by without the announcement of a gadget claiming to be 'the world's first' that solves a problem we don't actually have. Here I've listed some gadgets which are perhaps a little before their time, that would be great but for the limits of current technology or that simply should not have been invented at all.

The Smartbe 'intelligent stroller'

Being a parent myself I appreciate that a child's first years can be tiring. The *Smartbe* is being marketed as the first intelligent stroller in the world, employing motion-tracking sensors to follow you wherever you go, providing hands-free strolling or an assisted push. In addition to the motor the stroller also includes wireless speakers, a bottle warmer, on-board heating, directional signals, internal/external cameras along with an anti-theft alarm. The battery lasts for about 6 hours and it can also charge your phone. My concern would be that, despite all of the on-board sensors and logic, there is no substitute for due care and attention, so what if an accident were to occur because the stroller was in full automatic mode and the parent wasn't paying attention? And at over $3,000 for a relatively short-term use device I think I'd rather pocket the cash and burn a few extra calories.

The Air Umbrella

The problem with the traditional umbrella that we've known and loved for literally centuries is that it can be difficult to open and close, drips everywhere and can turn inside-out in windy weather. The air umbrella solves this by creating a curtain of air, blown out from the top of its long thin shaft to shield you from the rain. However, the problem with the air umbrella is that it weighs 800 grams (twice the weight of a normal umbrella), has a battery life of about 30 minutes and costs about $120. I'm also not sure how I'd feel about walking down the road holding something akin to a light sabre that's making a hissing noise, although the makers suggest that you won't hear it above the rain shower it's protecting you from. If the battery life can be improved to a few hours and they can chop the weight down a bit then I think this would be a great advancement on an age-old gadget, but for now I think I'll continue to struggle with the existing technology on a windy, rainy day.

The Digitsole Smartshoes

If you ever wanted a pair of shoes similar to those worn by Marty McFly in *Back to the Future* now's your chance. Digitsole have released a range of smart shoes, which are Bluetooth enabled and can warm your feet. Including front and rear lights on some models, they are self-lacing, they'll track how many steps you've taken and also tell you how many calories you've burned. There's also an app for both iOS and Android. The batteries last around six hours, after which you can charge them wirelessly with what looks like a set of headphones for your shoes. The price? Around €350. You can also buy just the insoles to wear with your existing footwear, but at €199 for those alone you may want to just stick to an extra pair of socks.

The Smart Belt

The *Welt* from heavyweight tech giant Samsung looks like a regular leather belt but is equipped with sensors and an alarm. The *Welt* (wellness belt, in case you were wondering) aims to alert you if you've been sitting too long or if your waistline is expanding too much. I don't need a belt to tell me that – I'm married! This product was showcased at CES in 2016 but as part of Samsung's Creative Lab project. As a result it may not actually become a consumer product – let's hope not.

Sensorwake Alarm Clock

Rather than waking you up by the traditional method of noise the *Sensorwake* alarm clock uses small disposable capsules that emit a scent at a predetermined time. Choose from the smell of croissants, espresso, seaside, lush jungle, chocolate or peppermint. Each capsule is good for '30 awakenings', but I fear nothing short of something akin to 'eau de vomit' would rouse me from a deep slumber. The *Sensorwake* will set you back around $90, and then of course you have to buy the capsules once the initial supply runs out.

The Solafeet foot tanner

Yes, this is indeed a real product! Apparently a female golfer complained to her husband that she suffered white feet from wearing golfing shoes and socks with shorts, which didn't look good when she went out for the evening in a dress. He invented the *Solafeet* ST-400. This device looks like a foot spa and requires around 15 minutes each day for a couple of weeks to provide a tan. It also apparently delivers other health benefits such as vitamin D and D3 and helps the body to produce serotonin – the good mood drug. The cost is $269. Alternatively, after a round of golf you could just sit outside and put your feet up.

The TV Hat

Billed as a portable private theatre, the TV hat is essentially a baseball cap with an extended 'bill' and three-sided blackout area front, left and right, and a clear pouch for your mobile phone to slide into. Between the phone and your eyes (which is about a 15-20cm gap) is a sliding lens to allow you to get the focus right. According to the maker's website this was developed for astronauts, but their marketing focus on their website suggests that its target audience are more likely to want to watch 'adult entertainment' on it.

The Yum and Done Smart Spoon for kids

This Bluetooth-enabled smart spoon works in conjunction with an app for your phone or tablet along with what looks like a glove puppet for your electronic device, with the ultimate aim of trying to goad them into eating vegetables. Slap your phone inside the critter and the screen shows through holes to animate the mouth and eyes. Each time the child eats their veggies they are greeted by sounds of encouragement, – further cementing their desire from an even younger age to spend more time playing with a touch screen device.

The Wocket Smart Wallet

This actually sounds like a great idea. It's a standalone smart wallet that can scan not just your credit cards, but loyalty cards and even gift cards. It uses a touch screen with e-ink, does not need to sync with your phone and allows either pin or voice control for authorisation. My two big concerns with this are that firstly it simply won't be accepted by some stores, and secondly I'm not sure I'd trust such a device with every single one of my payment methods stored on it for fear of theft or their security being compromised.

The Inner Selfie Stick

You'll be glad that I didn't include a picture with this one! The *Inner Selfie Stick* is basically an endoscope for the iPhone, allowing you to provide the ultimate, intimate image of your inner workings. Connecting via the Lightning port, the VGA resolution camera head is 14mm wide, an eye-watering 2m long and usefully ships with 100ml of lubricant. The makers also recommend purchasing 'one head per orifice'. Ironically the camera is also compatible with FaceTime, Apple's face-to-face video conferencing app, although I suspect any calls made using this would be a rather one-sided conversation. On the plus side it'll take your Instagrams to a whole (or should that be 'hole') new level.

The Cardboard Home Cinema

While *Google Cardboard* was a great idea and brought VR to the masses, the *Cardboard Home Cinema* takes this idea and makes everything that was right about it wrong. Imagine a 33 x 45 x 31cm box with one open side for your face, the inside painted black and a place to strap your phone 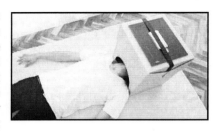 or tablet. Now imagine having to lie on the floor to use it and paying £25 for that privilege. This was actually successfully crowd-funded on the Japanese version of Kickstarter, but unlike *Google Cardboard* you can't take advantage of the gyroscope to look around – you'll just be lying on the floor with a box on your head, waiting for someone to trip over you or to be committed.

Stresstickles

Stress balls designed to look like.... No. Just no.

Appendix C – The future of gadgets

While I don't profess to be a futurologist I can recall a number of occasions in the past where I've discussed with friends what direction a particular technology might be going in and have been reasonably on target. It's a given that technology will get smaller and faster, but what else can we expect in the next few years?

Fitness trackers are already mainstream, but I believe you can expect a great deal more data over and above the basics of steps taken, calories burned and heart rate. There are already products in beta test that are not far removed from the Star Trek 'Tri-corder', being able to scan the body's vital functions in seconds. It's not too much of a stretch to imagine a patch containing a myriad of sensors that can check general health indicators or specific medical issues, such as blood sugar level for diabetics, thus removing the need for regular finger-prick blood tests. Your heart could be monitored with such accuracy that days or weeks before a potential heart attack you could be notified of a problem. (That'd be a great alert to receive on your phone!) Diagnosis of problems could be much quicker, such as stroke. Fixing them will become easier as well, using nanotechnology – controllable robots that could be injected into the bloodstream and directed towards a blocked artery in order to clear it, for example.

The smartphone will only continue to tighten its grip on your life as it becomes the hub for your Internet of Things devices around the home or car, which of course exacerbates the problem considerably if it gets lost, stolen or broken. My advice: don't sell that old phone – keep it in a drawer as a backup! You can always use it as a security camera in the meantime.

A few scaremongers regularly predict that robots will take most of our jobs. Well, it hasn't happened yet, and we've had robots in manufacturing for decades. In fact Mercedes Benz actually traded robots for humans recently as people were better at handling the change and complexity of key customisation options for its S-Class model.

As a rule, technology tends to create employment rather than reduce it. What generally happens when new technologies go mainstream – either in business or at a consumer level – is that new opportunities present themselves and new markets spring up. Look at the mobile phone industry as an example – in addition to several mobile stores on every high street there is a big industry to supply accessories and the apps industry is absolutely huge.

The wearable technology market is starting to blossom but to my mind there are certain elements that hold it back – namely battery life and component size. Take smart watches – I personally opted for the *Pebble* watch, a crowd-funded smart watch that does not possess quite the same array of sensors as the Apple, Samsung or Sony watches. Nor does it include Apple's beautiful touch screen. What it does have, however, is up to 10 days battery life and *just* enough smart functionality (such as notifications, step tracking and vibration alert) to be useful. Do I want to play games on my watch or be able to start my car from it? No. At the moment I feel that the smart watch market is still trying to find its feet, with every mobile app developer bringing out a smart watch extension. It's a solution trying to meet a problem that doesn't really exist. As the market matures with the same level of adoption as smartphones then we'll start to see real killer apps appear such as biometric identification using your heartbeat.

The wonder material graphene will make its presence felt to a much wider audience. This super material is incredibly thin, strong, lightweight and super-conductive, but still expensive and difficult to manufacture in large quantities. Companies are already working to include it into battery technology with the ultimate aim of a phone that will charge in minutes and run for days or even weeks. Flexible technology is a real possibility – a live map that you can just fold up and put in your pocket, not dissimilar to the newspapers from the Harry Potter movies.

Continuing on the energy theme, areas such as harnessing solar power will continue to improve, both in efficiency and size. Scientists have already developed a clear solar panel, with the short term aim of including it into a watch screen. Roll forward a few years and you could be driving (or being driven by) a car that self-charges through the windscreen. A conspiracy theorist might suggest that the oil companies would sit on this one for a few years though...

For me the biggest concern going forward is not AI (artificial intelligence), as some have predicted, but the old thorn of security. In recent years there have been so many high-profile security hacks from companies that we should be able to trust with our data – Sony, TalkTalk (3 times, no less!), BT and eBay to name but a few. At the moment these thefts have centred around names, addresses, emails and financial information. If you now throw biometrics into that mix, with thieves being able to perhaps mimic your stolen biometric data then we might lose what could be the only way to prove who we actually are.

AI in the home will be an increasingly important factor in our lives moving forward, as our tech learns our preferences and tries to better meet our needs. In a fully connected home you might envisage a situation where you go on holiday and the home prepares itself automatically for your return, ordering food for the fridge, setting the heating and reading your messages (in order of importance) as you walk through the door. It could even tell you who tried to visit you while you were away using facial recognition.

George Orwell was certainly right, and I expect Big Brother will continue to watch over us all, and this will become easier as we leave a greater digital footprint. I'm expecting a day in the not-too-distant future when instead of being offered a modest discount on my car insurance if I fit a tracker to my car (the 'soft sell' approach), I will find myself pressured into accepting the tracker as it becomes prohibitively expensive *not* to have one or, worse still, mandatory to include it. Take that one stage further and you could arrive home after a particularly exhilarating drive to be notified that you've been automatically disqualified! One positive automotive development would be the ability for a car to be able to assess whether the driver is able and authorised to drive it, e.g. do they have a license, are they insured and have they been drinking, with the car preventing you from driving off if those conditions are not met.

To my mind I think we're still a way off from having our own robot butlers at home. For one thing voice-recognition technology is still not 100% accurate, but that is dwarfed by the complexities of producing a robot that can interact as delicately with its environment as we do. Imagine today's robots trying to dust your mantlepiece! Instead in the short term we will continue to see a convergence of technologies in the home, more sensors crammed into 'traditional' devices and more communication between them.

Lower-powered or environmentally-powered devices and internet access in even the most remote of locations could revolutionise industry. Take farming. Farmers would not only be able to track their flock of sheep but could also monitor their health, getting early warnings for diseases that ordinarily might wipe out their entire livestock. In London pigeons have already been used to track pollution using backpacks fitted with GPS and sensors capable of measuring various gasses with the results instantly (and ironically) being tweeted.

I touched on health and fitness earlier. When I was born you would hope to get your 'three score years and ten' in this life before you shuffle off your mortal coil, yet those born today can easily expect to live into their 90s. An ageing population brings other problems, both physical and mental. Hopefully medical advancements will curtail the growth of age-related mental problems such as dementia, but I can see that materials such as graphene could be used to build 'exoskeletons' to assist with mobility. We're not specifically talking full body suits here, but perhaps near skin-tight designs that can take the strain from the knees, arms or spine. Couple that with small motors and flexible 'muscles' and you can create an external structure that can drastically enhance the body's own capabilities. Industrial-sized versions of such a device would transform any job that previously required say, a small fork-lift truck. Your local garden centre or DIY store staff would certainly benefit.

For all of the possible negatives I cannot help but be excited about the future of technology. When I was growing up in the 80s I felt that I was witnessing a technological revolution, as computers started to find their way into the home. The same was true of the internet. I remember a good friend of mine calling it a fad in the mid 1990s. I think we can all agree that the internet is here to stay, and it will continue to be the backbone by which all devices communicate, but the growth in devices using it autonomously rather than us checking email, browsing the web or streaming media will be exponential. We are again on the cusp of something truly wonderful.